The Supernatural Power of Music

A QUANTUM LEAP INTO WORSHIP

Len Mink

ACKNOWLEDGMENTS

Cathy Mink – Thank you for your unconditional love, patience, and unwavering faith. You are my shining light and an amazing gift from God.

Kenneth Copeland – For being my example of courage, faithfulness, and integrity.

Charles Capps & Kenneth Hagin – For teaching the bedrock realities of faith.

Father Tom Turnbull & Arthur Blessitt – For being at the right place at the right time.

To my children Carrie & Lenny – Who unselfishly allowed their father to travel the world to discover many of the revelations in this book.

Dr. Jack Hayford – We have many leaders, but few fathers.

Annette Capps – For striking the quantum tuning fork in my life.

Sheryl Riggs – Whose deep foundations in God's Word and exceptional literary gifts have helped bring this project before the eyes of millions.

Melanie Hemry – For turning chaos into order.

Rebecca Eubanks – For her artistic designs and modern-media gifts.

Andrea Murphy Photography – For your gift and calling behind the camera.

Dr. Mary Beth Policastro – For her heart for Israel and her deep insight into true worship.

Dale Mauck – The best I have ever seen in staging and lighting. Thank you for decades of backstage conversations about sound, light, and the quantum world.

Huge thanks to our special book partners who invested in this project. Your trust, partnership and faith in this exciting message will pay rich dividends in the life of every reader. Remember, God keeps good books!

BOUNDLESS

In humble awe I stand upon the edge of space and time.

This vast expanse by word, not chance,
sung from the Heart Divine.

From chaos, order; from darkness, light,
the outward worlds unfurled

Yet right behind our outbound gaze lie endless
inner worlds.

TABLE OF CONTENTS

A DIVINE PROCLAMATION

The Holy Spirit Indentifies Himself

I Am the Holy Spirit. I am the energy, the facilitator, the builder of worlds that are launched by divine utterance. I obey the "let there be…" command from the Father, from the Son and from you. I Am the builder of worlds, both visibly expansive and unseen. I turn words into worlds.

I Am the muscle of the angelic host. I Am the great Convicter and Convincer. I Am the guide and mapmaker for destinies. I Am the delivery power and installer of shalom and every other facet of the Father and Son into the human spirit.

Practice my presence in worship, in the Word, and with each other. Hop aboard my abilities; I have qualified you to partake of the fullness of my Blessings. For to abandon the confines of your self-imposed limitations and to embrace My limitless power *is* the pathway to divine supply and everlasting joy.

Len Mink
May 17, 2019

CHAPTER ONE

IN THE BEGINNING

In the very beginning, the Eternal God—the Unbegun One—stepped out onto the precipice of time and eternity, and through divine frequencies, He sang. His song gave birth to all matter, and every dimension was created. Because God *is* love, He sang a love song.

The words of the song said, "Let there be light." When its crescendo peaked at its highest note, a burst of light exploded into being. His Voice sped through the dark at the speed of light.

Balls of fire and ice shone bright in the deepest darkness. A cloud of dust, which He sang as a nebula, formed a blood-red center surrounded by emerald fans of light. It danced to life and formed a solar system.

Asteroids and comets shot across the universe, singing back to their Creator. Swirls of color erupted. The Milky Way pirouetted into its place. Every particle of light danced to life and sang a song of its own. Songs of worship echoed at the speed of light.

The sun and the moon bowed to His majesty as they obeyed His command. Planets took form. Mars glowed red. Jupiter appeared, painted with swirls and stripes of color. Earth rocked on its axis until it locked in place. Seas and waters separated the solid masses. Trees clapped their hands in song. Rocks formed a rhythm of their own. All of creation joined His song.

A massive cosmic saturation of sound shot forth as praise to God. Every created thing harmonized in His chorus.

Many learned rabbis in Israel believe there is scriptural evidence that God not only spoke "Let there be," but *sang* the worlds into existence. From this perspective music was downloaded into all of creation so that everything created had embedded within it the ability to sing a praise response back to God.

No wonder the Bible says in the Old Testament, "The morning stars sang together for joy at the work of his hands" (Job 38:7) and Jesus said in the New Testament, "If [the people] keep quiet, these stones will start shouting" (Luke 19:40, CEV).

Physicists explain that our universe is expanding at the speed of light. Science suggests that it shows signs of acceleration beyond the speed of light. His words and musical notes have never stopped creating.

"The morning stars sang together
for joy at the work of his hands"
– (Job 38:7)

The Creative Power of Sound

It's interesting that all matter was created by sound – the sound of His Voice. That sound created light. Light was created before the sun, which came into being on the fourth day.

How did that work? We'll discuss it later. For now, just know that music plays a major role in creation, both then and now.

Growing up in the highlands of Virginia I learned to play guitar and sing the familiar folk songs of that area. These songs were saturated with history, humor, faith, and passion.

One Sunday afternoon I was playing and singing with friends and had leaned my guitar against the wall next to where I was seated. All of a sudden I heard it! My guitar was making sound all by itself. The strings were picking up the frequencies of the other stringed instruments being played across the room. I learned later that this is called sympathetic vibration. Even though I was very young, I grasped the concept that this was somehow related to God. Eventually I came to realize that my life should sympathetically resonate to the frequencies of God and allow them to flow through me to others. This ever-abiding fire in my bones has been a living reality now for many decades in my desire to be a conduit for the glory and love of God to pass through me to the hearts of other people.

As a singer and a songwriter, I struggled one day to find a melody to build around a new song I was writing. I was looking for a musical expression to convey to the listener my personal story of coming to faith in Jesus. I had the basic feel of the song, but I was struggling to grasp a tangible melody to build the song around.

It was a glorious fall afternoon, and the window in my study was open. I gazed outside, watching leaves of gold, orange, and crimson wave in the gentle breeze. Distracted from my song, I noticed a stunning red cardinal in the tree. He was so regal that I stopped to enjoy the moment.

Outside, I'd stacked firewood against the side of the house up to the bottom casement of the window. As if on cue, the cardinal fluttered to the top of the woodpile closest to the window. Then he turned to face me, looking right at me.

He paused, seeming to wait until he had my full attention. Then he sang a beautiful line of notes with tempo, syncopation and expression.

"Wow!" I thought, *"That was beautiful!"*

He stared me down. It felt like he was trying to tell me something. Then he hopped closer to the window and sang it again.

That's when it hit me. *That was the melody I'd been searching for!* It was perfect in every way. It was even in the perfect key.

I wrote down the melody while it was fresh and played it on my guitar. In a moment of holy inspiration, the entire song—music and lyrics—flowed out of me. The song in its entirety was completed in less than 15 minutes. It became the title song for my CD, "Free in the Name."

As I sat there, stunned, I thought of another scripture. "But ask the beasts, and they will teach you; the birds of the heavens, and they will tell you" (Job 12:7 ESV).

Biomusicologists argue that not only are the sounds of some animals pleasing, but they are also made up of the same musical language that humans use. Whales, for example, use many of the musical concepts found in human music, including similar rhythms, phrase lengths, and song structure. These similarities, the *Science* magazine writers maintain, "prove that these marine mammals are inveterate composers."

The writers also point to birds as musicians, noting that bird songs follow rhythmic patterns and pitches that are in tune with human music. Birds not only create vocal sound, but some also add percussion to their songs.

Having been raised in the wild and beautiful highlands of Virginia, I had a good grip on nature, animals, weather, and the whole great outdoors experience. But that day, my sensitivity to the literal meaning of Psalm 66 took on new meaning. "All the earth worships you and sings praises to you; they sing praises to your name."

Psalm 50:11 says, "I know all the birds on the hills, and all that moves in the field is mine" (ESV).

That day, the word *songbird* took on a whole new meaning for me!

The point I'm making is that not only did *sound* create the universe and everything in it, but all of creation continues to sing in worship to God.

If I were not a physicist, I would probably be a musician.
I often think in music. I live my daydreams in music.
I see my life in terms of music.
– Albert Einstein 1894-1955

My Journey

As a youngster, I craved to travel the world. My hunger for knowledge was so great that while in grade school, I read the encyclopedia from Aardvark through Zweig. I pored over every issue of *National Geographic*.

"That boy has wanderlust," Mama said.

For as long as I could remember, I'd wanted to travel and sing. Sometimes I sang for pocket change. Often, I sang for free. Most of my experience was centered around acoustic folk music. Year after year, I developed my singing and guitar playing by participating in church choirs, fiddlers' conventions, bluegrass festivals, and folk groups.

Later, in the Navy, I sang in the Blue Jacket Choir. Afterwards, I played and sang anywhere, anytime. It's not that I wouldn't do anything else. It's more like I didn't want to do anything else.

I was asked to be a guest singer at a country/gospel/bluegrass/folk event in Logan, West Virginia. Of course, it paid nothing. I was in Logan and flat broke two days before my three-song debut. On foot and hungry, I walked down the river road to a fast food drive-in. I had my guitar and backpack on as I went to the rear door of the drive-in to ask the manager if there was any work I could do in exchange for a meal.

As I look back on that experience, the manager reminds me of Polly Holliday's character, Flo, on the 70's sitcom *Alice*. I told her I was in town for the music event at the Veterans' Memorial in two days. She got a mischievous glint in her eye. "If you'll take your guitar and walk around the cars of all my drive-in customers and serenade them for half an hour, I'll feed you whatever you'd like."

And then, as if on cue, it started to rain.

Dripping wet, I sang, I ate, I cried.

Something inside me clicked that day: *Sing = Eat.*

That led to several such events, talent shows, and festivals. I learned a lot of survival skills on the road. With frequent stops at my parents' house for a good meal and a decent bed, I strayed further and further from home.

In 1968, I found out that none of the singers slated to sing for a March of Dimes Telethon in Knoxville, Tennessee, were interested in singing from three until four o'clock in the morning. I grabbed the opportunity. All I had to do was sing a lot and ask viewers to call in and donate. I enjoyed myself, and I guess it showed. This was my first appearance on television.

The Call

After I finished my segment, the stage manager told me I had a phone call. The man on the phone worked for a major television broadcasting company. He was in a hotel, unable to sleep, so he'd flipped on the television while I was singing. He invited me to meet him for breakfast.

We met, ate, and talked. Three hours later, we flew to Cincinnati for an on-air audition. Afterwards he said, "Don't call us. We'll call you." Then we went our separate ways.

Six months passed with no word from him. I got a job at a gas station. I was changing a tire on a big truck when my mother called. She gave me a number to call in Cincinnati.

It was the television studio offering me a job.

I went home to pack one small bag and my guitar. I borrowed my mother's old car until I could afford to get one of my own. I left for Cincinnati that day with bald tires, one suit, two shirts, one tie, one pair of holey shoes, and $62.00.

I lived at the YMCA for a couple of weeks as I went to my television job as assistant janitor.

I worked at many different jobs at the CBS affiliate station and learned much about television. Over time, a band was hired, a set was built and "The Len Mink Show" was born. It did very well in the ratings. Before long, the show was syndicated nationwide. I knew I'd succeeded when "The Tonight Show" audience gave me a standing ovation. Then and there, Johnny Carson invited me to return for another guest appearance.

I appeared on "The Merv Griffin Show" and "The Mike Douglas Show" and performed as guest soloist in thirty-two concerts with the Cincinnati Symphony Orchestra. I sang in concerts with people like Itzhak Perlman, Yo-Yo Ma, Miles Davis, Cannonball Adderley, Joe Williams, Lena Horne, Gerry Mulligan, Doc Severinsen and many others.

I did a pilot show with CBS for my own network program. This boy from the mountains was doing all right!

During that time, I met Cathy, a model whom I'd seen in fashion magazines. We each realized as we dated that there was something missing from our lives, both as a couple and as individuals. The more we searched for the answer, the more desperate we felt. Each of us came face to face with the glaring truth. The more we achieved in our careers, the emptier we felt. In time we broke up.

God always sends someone to get your attention. That person in our story was Ken Bagwell, an associate producer at the television station where Cathy and I worked. One Monday morning Ken showed up for work, but there was something different about him. We quizzed him regarding his very noticeable change. He replied simply, "Over the weekend I invited Jesus into my heart and was born again." He had a noticeable peace and joy about him, and we wanted it. Over time, he answered our many questions, always with scripture.

A Man with a Cross

With Ken in charge of production many Christian guests began popping up. One such guest was Arthur Blessitt. Arthur had written a book called *Turned On to Jesus* and opened a night club in California on the Sunset Strip to reach hippies, bikers, and drug addicts with the good news of the Gospel. Arthur began to tour, carrying an 80-pound wooden cross. When he came to Cincinnati, he ended up at our television station. His interview was riveting, and love shone brightly from his eyes.

I walked Arthur out of the studio after the show. As we passed through the darkened news studio he paused to shake my hand. Grasping my hand, he dropped down on one knee. He bowed his head and prayed for me OUT LOUD. He prayed that I would experience the love of Jesus and find purpose and fulfillment. I was speechless. We walked to his van, and I just stood there stunned as he drove off. I had a strange feeling that my life was about to change dramatically.

One day as I drove home in my new Mercedes, the emptiness in my soul overwhelmed me. It felt like the Grand Canyon. Having my own television show hadn't filled it. Screaming fans hadn't filled it. Owning a Mercedes hadn't filled it. A beautiful girlfriend hadn't filled it.

At home, I went inside feeling like a walking dead man. I pulled out my double-barreled shotgun. Loading both barrels, I sat on the side of my bed and positioned the barrels under my chin. I put my thumb on the trigger. Ready to die, I whispered, "God help me."

Instantly the room exploded with a supernatural peace and a palpable presence.

Amazed, I put down the gun and cried, "You're here aren't you? I'm not leaving this room until I hear from You!"

Trembling, I sat. I waited. Thirty minutes later, I heard a knock on the door. It was Cathy. I hadn't seen her for 10 weeks. She stood there with a little psychedelic-colored New Testament in her hand. (Arthur Blessitt had given it to her.)

"Len," she said, "I found what we've been looking for!"

"What?"

"Jesus!"

"Where did you find Jesus?"

"At Barney's Hamburger Stand last night with Ken Bagwell!"

"What was Jesus doing at Barney's Hamburger Stand?" I asked.

"Saving me!" she said, and burst into tears.

Cathy shared her story and several scriptures and then went home.

The Dream

I fell asleep one Friday night in October, still trying to juggle my emotions and make sense of all this new revelation from Cathy. I had the most vivid dream I'd ever experienced.

I dreamed I was walking downhill along an unpaved, muddy road. I came to a rundown old shack. It reminded me of the ones near where I grew up in Virginia, in the coal fields. I stopped in front of the shack.

An old man sat in a rocking chair on the porch, wearing dirty bib overalls and a filthy tee-shirt. Deep wrinkles, like the grooves in a pecan, creased his face. His fingernails were stained and dark. He appeared never to have bathed in his life.

We locked eyes. I felt frozen, unable to move. Those laser eyes!

Never breaking eye contact, he lifted an old fiddle to his grey-bearded cheek and held the bow in his hand. Then he paused for a few seconds, just staring at me.

It seemed an eternity.

He played a rendition of "Amazing Grace" that was more beautiful than anything I'd ever heard. The music echoed in every molecule of my being. I didn't just hear it. I *felt* it. It pierced my heart in the gentlest way. I felt exhilarated. I felt healed in a way I couldn't describe. I felt touched in the deepest recesses of my soul. I awoke sobbing.

It was Saturday morning, October 16, 1971 – a day that would change my life forever. Later that morning, Cathy and I walked into a Christian bookstore so she could buy a Bible and some other books. Little did I know that God had set an ambush for me. Waiting inside was Father Tom Turnbull, a born-again, Spirit-filled, turned on to Jesus Episcopal priest.

I'd been so moved by my dream the night before that I asked Father Tom what he thought it meant. In a voice filled with love, choosing his words with care he said, "The old man was Jesus. He was filthy because He bore your sins, your shame, your torment and your sickness on the cross. The song, 'Amazing Grace' was a musical depiction of His love and sacrifice for you. He would have given His life for you if you'd been the only person on earth. He knew that it would take a song to reach you. He spoke to you through music.

"He arose from the grave, having conquered death for all who will believe. He's alive. He loves you so much and wants you to invite Him into your heart."

Within the hour, I knelt and prayed in that Christian bookstore, giving my life to Jesus.

I was born again, made new, and radically saved by the grace of God, washed in Jesus' blood. As I left the bookstore, I knew I was taking my first steps into my new life.

I paused with my hand on the doorknob. "Lord, what do I do now?" I whispered.

His reassuring voice within me responded, *"Len, wherever you go, whatever you do, just create an atmosphere for Me to be Myself. I'll do the rest."*

That day began my lifelong song to the Music Maker.

A couple of months later, I had a shocker. I was diagnosed with a terminal blood disease. Friends began to talk to me about healing. A fan visited me in the hospital and brought me a copy of Kathryn Kuhlman's book, *I Believe in Miracles*. By the time I finished reading it, I believed in them too. God healed me in a miraculous way, and the doctors then gave me a clean bill of health. I sang at many of Kathryn Kuhlman's meetings and appeared on her television program.

Cathy and I were married in 1972. We began to grow in the Lord, traveling everywhere to sing and tell our story. As we traveled, we listened to Christian radio and heard a teacher named Kenneth E. Hagin. Our spirits resonated with him. In 1973 we attended the very first Kenneth Hagin Campmeeting in Tulsa, Oklahoma. I was surprised and honored to be asked to sing. In coming years I sang at all but one of Brother Hagin's Campmeetings. It was there that we met Kenneth and Gloria Copeland. That led to the invitation to lead worship in the Kenneth Copeland meetings across the globe and helping establish his television ministry outreach. My leading KCM worship stretched to over 42 years!

I've appeared in many Christian television productions: *The 700 Club, Help Line, Turning Point, 100 Huntley Street, PTL, TBN, The Believer's Voice of Victory,* and countless others. I was also honored to share ministry platforms with Lester Sumrall, Morris Cerullo, James Robison, Demos Shakarian, T.L. Osborne, Charles Capps, Jerry Savelle, Jesse Duplantis, Creflo Dollar, Keith Moore, Bill Winston, and dozens of others.

Today Cathy and I have our own television program called *Len and Cathy* on DirecTV, channel 377. It is produced by the TCT Television Network, founded by Garth & Tina Coonce. The program can also be seen on Apple TV, Amazon Fire, Roku, You Tube, Truli, Android TV, the TCT Mobile App, iTunes Video Podcasts and many cable networks. It can also be viewed from our website at LenandCathyMink.com.

We often host *The Roadshow* on the Oasis Radio Network, founded by David and Sharon Ingles. I am the writer and voice behind Gospel Duck, reaching thousands of children around the world. We are also members of The Tribe of Judah motorcycle ministry.

Some things, however, haven't changed. I still love to travel the world. I still have an insatiable curiosity. My journey has taken me from the study of the universe in all its majestic glory to the deep exploration of music and the study of quantum physics. I invite you to join me on this exciting adventure as we explore the *supernatural power of music*

CHAPTER TWO

A QUANTUM LEAP

Think of the miracles in the Bible. The parting of the Red Sea. The walls of Jericho falling. Jesus turning water into wine. His appearing inside a locked room after the resurrection.

For years, skeptics wrote these miracles off as fiction. That changed as God began releasing the revelation of quantum physics. Today, many scholars say that every miracle in the Bible can be explained through quantum physics.

What *is* quantum physics? In its simplest form, it's the fundamental theory in physics which describes nature at its smallest scale of energy, such as atoms and subatomic particles.

It all started with the words, "Let there be light."

Quantum particles, called light particle waves, form atoms. Atoms form molecules. Molecules form objects, both living and nonliving. Therefore, material objects are made up of particles.

Taking it a step further, they are also made up of the forces that hold particles together. According to quantum mechanics, light is the force that keeps electrons connected to the core or nucleus of an atom. Atoms bond together making molecules. And molecules make objects.

Science confirms that all forms of matter are made up of *solidified light*.

For eons, the Biblical description of creation didn't make much natural sense. For instance, how could light exist before the sun?

Now, through quantum physics, we understand that *nothing* could exist without light first existing. Light is the force that holds all matter together. Interestingly enough, it was sound, "Let there be," that gave birth to light!

Sir Isaac Newton, the father of classical physics, is best known for his study of gravity and motion. From his work, we've learned that the universe works like a precise machine, making many things predictable and measurable.

Then the German physicist Max Planck began his experiments with light and what we now call quantum physics, quantum theory and quantum mechanics. These all include the study of subatomic particles.

There are deeper and deeper levels and layers of information and revelation being discovered on a regular basis. It's like having a big box with smaller boxes fitting inside each one. However, with subatomic particles, there is no end in sight.

One of Max Planck's well known discoveries was the double-slit experiment. In this study, he learned that light waves and light particles are affected by the presence of an onlooker.

Yes, you read those words right.

When an observer was present, light waves collapsed and became light particles. Being observed changed light from one state to another. That means light acts like an organism, *knowing* when it's being observed.[1] Light is not only energy, but it seems to possess *personality*—an expression of divine origin.

In His sermon on the mount, Jesus said, "You are the light of the world..." (Matthew 5:14a).

If I could paraphrase that verse, it would read like this, "If you will be completely surrendered and available to me, I will transmit through you into the earth the incomparable power and all-sufficiency of My Father's love and ability."

In today's world of high-speed communication, fiber optics has changed the world in dramatic ways. Through shafts of glass, each no bigger than a human hair, light can carry data, video and audio files, with each fiber carrying many different streams of data on different frequencies—all at the same time.

Lasers are beams of highly concentrated light able to be used to perform brain surgeries or to cut huge metal slabs like hot butter.

If you want to find the secrets of the universe,
think in terms of energy, frequency and vibration.
– Nikola Tesla

Consider the revelation that an onlooker's presence can change the very form of light. This sounds like expectation (faith). Through this revelation, we can understand that Jesus was saying, "Your very presence, prayers, and participation *change everything around you.* It gives Me access to express the Father's love through you, a yielded conduit, with one end attaching to the supply of heaven and the other end aimed at needy humanity."

Even though the infinite variety of our unique personalities aids in creating endless ways to share God's love, it is imperative that we become a pass-through pipeline. Yet we must not change or taint the divine frequencies coming through us to their Holy Spirit-led destinations.

Subatomic Particles

There are dozens of subatomic particles that have been discovered in the last 50 years. As technology and the world of the spirit interface more and more, these discoveries are increasing.

Because there is so much data in these mini building blocks, time and space won't allow full discussion of them here. However, there are a few revelations that are noteworthy, that will expand our horizons and thrill our spirits.

One of the earliest, discovered decades ago, is the quark. Researchers soon noticed that this particle wasn't a particle at all—at least not all the time.

Most subatomic entities have common characteristics of operation in their universally acknowledged "circular, orbital behavior." They move in a circular motion. This is a pattern throughout the cosmos. The quark, however, sometimes takes on a *wave form*. At other times, it acts as *both* a particle and a wave at the same time.

This is now called the wave-particle duality. It has become a fundamental tenet of quantum mechanics. The first thing to understand is that these changing wave forms allow matter to transport from one place to another, even moving through objects.

The tiny micro world is every bit as exciting as the big cosmic picture. It holds valuable treasures for those who continue to plumb the depths of discovery and understanding. When we tap into them, we find that humans are the focal point of the grandest expression of life and power imaginable.

A New Psalm

> *"The Genesis utterance, both spoken and sung,*
> *The original sounds from the Unbegun One,*
> *Unfurled the whole universe, far flung or small,*
> *Immutable evidence, love gift for all!*

Jesus the Son, by whom everything came,
Has given His children the use of His Name.
Divine frequencies released from the heart,
Bring Genesis light, make darkness depart.

The Word, first God-spoken, then written by men,
Is declared by us now again and again

To push back the shadows of blindness and fear,
To make known God's greatness,

Salvation is here!

©Len Mink
July 30, 2016

Another captivating aspect of this is called quantum entanglement. This allows the actions by one particle to affect another particle to delay the *choice* of whether to be a particle or a wave.

Wow. A choice? Do these subatomic particles have choices?

Obviously, they do, because they are living, divinely designed fragments of matter that are meant to become what the Designer intended. It seems that *choice* goes deeper than we thought.

The quark, in wave form, is thought to be a sound wave. Could it be the sonic signature of the Supreme Creator Himself, indelibly imprinted upon and within *all* matter, no matter how small?

Another tiny player, the Higgs-Boson particle, is sometimes referred to as the "God particle." It is a recently discovered particle that is responsible for giving all other particles their mass or substance.

The Bible tells us, "Now faith is the substance of things hoped for, the evidence of things not seen" (Hebrews 11:1).

In Mark 11:23, Jesus says that if we speak to a mountain (this could be a tumor or a disease) and command it to be removed and do not doubt in our hearts (expectation/faith) but believe that what we expect and speak shall come to pass, we will have it. Does the movement of these sub-atomic particles explain this scripture? Is Jesus telling us we can determine the behavior of these tiny material actors?

Another quantum theory, the elusive "string theory," is a gravity related postulation that envisions the possibility of the shape of subatomic particles being more like parallel strings vibrating at different frequencies. The space between the strings is what we call mass or matter. The violin maker Antonio Stradivari had the right idea!

In Psalm 33:3 we read, "Sing to Him a new song; play skillfully on the strings, with loud shouts!" (ESV).

Whether we initially understand these concepts or not, it is becoming clear that as we delve deeper into this amazing micro universe, we will always find God the Father, God the Son, and God the Holy Spirit busy at work, revealing God's personality, power and materiality. With each discovery, we will find God's grace, acceptance, and provision waiting there for us. There is no escaping His eternal passion for you, the object of His never-ending love.

A Spiritual Language

What does all this have to do with music? Quite a lot as it turns out.

Music is an eternal, spiritual, and cosmic link between the natural world and the spirit world. We, as humans, are speaking spirits. That's how we're like God. Music is the spiritual language that unites the physical and the spiritual. It's amazing that music can transcend all limitations.

When you sing a song—or say something in music—words are carried in a container of frequencies, vibrations, and waveforms. They can lubricate and change the shape of that word, and cause it to slip into the deep places where only God's Word can go.

The word *psalm* in the original Hebrew means "songs raving and boasting about God." The Psalms are sometimes arranged to achieve certain end results. For instance, primarily in Jewish worship, one arrangement is called *Sayings of Gold*. If you recite them in a certain order, supernatural things occur.

Another arrangement, called the *Hallel*, is where we get the word hallelujah. It comes from the words *hallel* and *Yah*. *Yah* is Yahweh, God's Old Testament name. *Hallel* means to "command praise to the Most High God."

Hallel has a couple of sub-meanings. One of them is "utter and complete light exploding in the face of utter and complete darkness." So, when you say the word hallelujah, you're engaging in God's quantum language. In the most literal of terms, you're saying, "Light, be!"

There's an old joke that's worth repeating: Two angels stood to one side and watched as God spoke and sang everything into existence. Wide-eyed and puzzled, one angel turned to the other and asked "How can something you can touch and see be real?"

Angels must be amused when they hear us questioning, "How can something you *can't* touch or see be real?"

In truth, there is a divine language that speaks to both the seen and the unseen world. That language is music.

The motherlode of everything that exists in our temporal world is within the realm of the spirit. Our five physical senses were given so that we could navigate through our physical world. Using these physical senses, however, to attempt to interpret the realities of the spirit world will always prove frustrating and unsuccessful. It would be like using your car's owner's manual to learn to fly an airplane. It won't work. One doesn't translate to the other.

Music awakens a person's hidden connection with God. There are hidden things that the Lord wants to reveal to us, and He often does so through a song. He will also give us certain songs to help us through difficult times.

Saul, the first king of Israel, shied away from that role, hiding among the baggage. He was so overwhelmed that when he was anointed king, Samuel had to assure him that his kingship was ordained by God.

Samuel gave him several signs that would prove that he was meant to be the first king of Israel. Among those signs, he was told that he would meet a band of traveling minstrels coming down from the high mountains. God would come upon them and they would prophesy. When that happened, the Spirit of God would come upon Saul. He would prophesy and become "another man."

God also used the power of music to convince Saul that he was to be king. In 1 Chronicles 25, we learn that Asaph, Heman and Jeduthun prophesied with the harp, the lute and the cymbal. Many people prophesied on instruments without saying a word. The music spoke, and the Holy Spirit imparted words, direction and deliverance to Saul and to the hearts of those listening.

The Work of the Minstrel

In 2 Kings, the third chapter, Israel faced a threat of being either enslaved or wiped out by the King of Moab. King Jehoram needed help, and he needed it quick. He turned to the King of Judah, Jehoshaphat, who agreed to help.

They got together and worked to develop a plan of defense. They came up with zip. Zero. Nothing. At long last, they decided that maybe they needed to hear from God.

One of the servants told them about the prophet Elisha. Elisha agreed to help. He had more miracles to his credit than anyone in the Old Testament. His prophetic accuracy was unparalleled. Still, he knew the need was great and that the word from God had to be sure.

That's when Elisha uttered the key element needed to turn a certain tragedy into a history changing victory.

He said, "Bring me a minstrel."

The Bible records that when the minstrel played, the hand of the Lord came on Elisha.

The Hebrew word for played is *nagan* (pronounced naw-gan). It means "to play a stringed instrument with the fingers of the hand." However, there are several places in scripture that suggest singing accompanied the playing.

As the musician played—and possibly sang—a prophetic download of gigantic proportions was released from the Spirit realm into the natural one. The plan was so wise, clever, and imaginative that Jehoshaphat shouted, "He's right! Elisha is right!"

It's evident from this passage that the musician knew what frequencies to play and sing for the revelation to be released to Elisha to give to the three kings.

The Delivering Power of Music

There are many instances of the supernatural influence of music and worship connecting earth to heaven. One such instance occurred when an evil spirit was on Saul as recorded in 1 Samuel 16:23. He would call for David to take a harp and play it with his hand.

Then Saul would become refreshed and well, and the distressing spirit would depart from him.

This passage reveals many facets of the power of music:

The influence of the music.

- The relationship between the king and the minstrel.

- The healing power of music upon the physical body, the mind, and the emotions.

- The soothing influence of music.

- The worth and worthiness of music.

- The truth is that we've hardly scratched the surface of this revelation. The immediate future holds exciting insights into bodies being healed and lives changed through music and song.

This story is a necessary reminder that worship leaders need to hear from God. They need intimate time in His presence. By faith, they must press in and believe for God's manifest presence when worship is offered to Him.

Remember, good or bad, whatever is in the heart of the worship director *will* transmit to the people. The words and the music may be magnificent in presentation, leaving hearers impressed with its grandeur. However, if those delivering the music have undesirable baggage on board, that baggage will download in varying degrees to the human spirits receiving it.

The amazing truth is that each one of us can come before the Lord in honesty and transparency and experience His cleansing grace and restoration, affirming the reality that our sins have been washed away by the supernatural power of Jesus' blood. When we walk in righteousness, His character will dominate our inner man. He'll be able to flow into us and through us to hungry souls everywhere.

Music is a Living Entity

*Music is the quill of the soul, expressing the most divine
aspect of the individual and collective humanity.
It records the past, it captures the present and it envisions
the future. Sometimes, it does all three at the same time.
– (Author unknown)*

Hebrews 13:8 says that Jesus Christ is the same yesterday, today and forever. God is the great I AM. He's never the I WAS or the I WILL BE.

Music takes all the dimensions of time and makes God present in each one.

Every time Israel, under David's leadership, expanded its expression of worship, several things happened. Their geographical boundaries expanded. Their wealth expanded. Miracles began manifesting.

Each time we step out in faith beyond the zone of comfortable predictability and start calling those things that be not as though they were, several things happen. Faith begins to work. Our boundaries expand. Wealth is expanded. Miracles begin manifesting.

Music isn't some sound *about* somebody. Music *is* Somebody. Music is a living entity.

CHAPTER THREE

THE BIG PICTURE

Since the dawn of time, man has articulated his belief in the power of a Being that created the cosmos and holds it together. Archeological findings are replete with evidence that even early Neolithic and Bronze-Age man was already expressing his belief in a Supreme Being through symbols, art, and carvings found all around the world.

God has revealed Himself as a triune God. It is translated Godhead in the Bible, but is more accurately rendered Godhood—the nature of God manifested (Deut. 6:4, James 2:19). He is not the austere, judgmental, unapproachable God found in religion, which is man's search for God. He has revealed Himself as One God, expressed in three distinct manifestations: the invisible, invincible Father; the visible and approachable Son, Jesus; and the indwelling, empowering Spirit.

God visited His creation at three distinct times. As God the Father, he walked and talked with Adam and Eve in the cool of the day (Genesis 3:8). As God the Son, He came to earth as Jesus Christ, clothed in a human body so that He could redeem fallen mankind, bringing us back into fellowship with Him. On Pentecost, He came as God the Holy Spirit, to live in residence within each believer and empower us with His abilities.

The creation is a tri-universe, comprising space, matter and time. Each is part of the others, and each part expresses the whole. Our universe is not *part* space, *part* matter, and *part* time. The three-part facets of God are not a triad, or even a trio, but a trinity. Each part is required in order to make the whole, yet within each distinct part is represented the complete person of God!

Space (the Father) is the omnipresent invisible backdrop for all that exists. Matter (Jesus, the Son) reveals the universe (the Godhead) in a visible, touchable, understandable form. Time (the Holy Spirit) is the entity by which the universe becomes understandable and applicable in events and experience.

Philip didn't understand this concept when he asked Jesus to show them the Father (John 14:8,9). Jesus answered, "Whoever has seen me has seen the Father."

The mathematics of the trinity is *not* 1+1+1=1.

It is rather 1x1x1=1.

The bottom line is that space is identified in one dimension, seen in the second dimension and experienced in the third dimension.

Time is future, present and past all at the same time.

In Exodus 3, God told Moses to go to Pharaoh and demand freedom for the children of Israel. In verse 14, God said, "Tell them I AM sent you." In the original Hebrew text, God said, "I will be what I will be!" (Whatever is needed.)

The future is the unseen, not-yet-lived part of time, manifested moment by moment in the present and understood and chronicled in the past.

These are a few examples of how the natural world mirrors and models the relationship between Father, Son, and Spirit. Water is the easiest to understand. Depending on the temperature, $H20$ can take the form of a solid (ice), a liquid (water) or a gas (steam). In all its forms, it's always $H20$.

Likewise, "Jesus Christ [is] the same, yesterday (past), today (present) and forever (future)," (Hebrews 13:8).

God's very name, I AM, indicates that He is present in our past, present in our present, and present in our future. He is reconciling and healing the past. He is kinetically using His might on our behalf in this present moment. He is standing with His arms open wide to us in our future, encouraging us to take a step forward in faith because His grace has already made the provision.

Gaining basic insight into these truths is vital in learning to cooperate with the way God does things.

Music can name the unnamable and
communicate the unknowable.
– Leonard Bernstein

Christianity, in its truest sense, is not a religion at all. It is a relationship. It's not just explosive, creative power. Love is involved.

As the epic love story of grace unfolds before our eyes in the Word of God and in creation around us, it becomes evident that we individual humans are the object of God's unfailing love. The family of God is not an organization. It's a living organism.

Hiking Along the Edge of the Quantum Frontier

Albert Einstein once said, "If I were not a physicist, I would probably be a musician. I often think in music. I live my daydreams in music. I see my life in terms of music."

The supernatural power of music can be fully comprehended only by understanding some of these basic principles of quantum physics.

I had a powerful time alone with God while on a backpacking trip. It was late at night, cold and crisp. No artificial light interrupted the view.

I stared at the night sky full of stars, moving satellites, the Milky Way, and constellations.

Then I heard it.

Deep on the inside of me, that familiar and powerful voice of love and tenderness spoke. The Lord spoke in a quiet tone as if the two of us were the only ones in the universe.

"I'm so blessed that you're enjoying My creation. I made it all for you. You're scanning outward into the deep expanses, trying to take it all in. That's My macro-universe.

"But looking the opposite way, inwardly into My creation, there is a micro-universe. It is My hidden, invisible world, equally as vast as the macro-universe. These are the concealed realms that build the visible world. I have saved most of that for the days that lie ahead, but be aware of it. Embrace it. It's the fine details of Who I Am. I Am Perfect Mathematics with a voice and a song. There is no end to Me in any direction."

Listening and looking, my thoughts exploded into a million different directions, macro and micro.

Quantum studies are very much like peeling layers of an onion as we explore what's underneath. It's like opening a box only to find a smaller one inside, then another and another.

Let's start with the largest building block in this micro-universe—the molecule.

Journey to the Center of the Earth

A molecule is the simplest structural unit of an element or compound. You might remember sixth grade science class and the drawings and models of different molecular structures. To help us understand, we'll take a quantum leap inside the molecule. Get ready to meet a side of God that you might never have known existed.

Even though objects we see in daily life – tables, chairs, rocks, trees, metal – appear to be inanimate, they are actually moving internally at such a high rate of speed that our eyes don't perceive it. The first question people ask is, "What holds it together?" As always, the Bible has the answer:

> For by Him all things were created that are in heaven and that are on earth, visible and invisible, whether thrones or dominions or principalities or powers.
>
> All things were created through Him and for Him. And He is before all things, and in Him all things consist, (Colossians 1:16-17).

He made the things we can see and the things we can't see, such as thrones, kingdoms, rulers, and authorities in the unseen realm. Everything was created through Him and for Him. He existed before anything else, and He holds all creation together.

In the King James Version of the Bible, Colossians 1:17 reads, "by him all things consist."

The Greek word for consist is *synesteken*, which suggests the properties of adhesion or glue. So, the most basic way to understand the cohesiveness of the universe is to realize that the Person of Jesus is the *cosmic glue that keeps everything from flying apart.*

Let's take a few minutes to slog through some basic facts to enhance our understanding. These molecular building blocks are made up of different ingredients. All matter is composed of elements. If you break *matter* down to its smallest components, you're left with individual elements. If you're breaking down a *molecule* into its smallest individual pieces, you get elements of the *same* type. If breaking down a *compound* to its smallest individual pieces, you're left with elements of *different* types.

Elements are also made up of something smaller: atoms. One atom of an element is the smallest piece of matter that can be measured. Of course, atoms are made up of something yet smaller, called subatomic particles. These, however, cannot be taken away from the atom without destroying the atom itself. Therefore, the atom is the smallest whole, stable piece of an element that still has the properties of that element.

Inside the nucleus (core) of an atom, there are two kinds of particles (pieces of matter). They are subatomic particles called protons and neutrons. Protons are positive charges, and neutrons have no charge. The nucleus at the center is positive.

We think of an atom's nucleus as a round sphere with a definite shape. In reality, the nucleus of an atom is a whirling conglomeration of particles.

Atoms are surrounded by negatively charged electrons. Just as batteries need to have positive and negative poles to function, an atom is held together by the pull between its positive nucleus and the negative electrons.

If the number of neutrons changes, then the nucleus of the atom can decay, although the overall atom still retains its chemical properties. But then it's called an isotope of the element. An isotope of an element has the same number of protons in its nucleus as other atoms of the element but a different number of neutrons.

Some of you are waiting for the sixth-grade, fourth period bell to ring and deliver you from all this weird science. Hang on, because we're almost there. This will all begin to make sense soon.

We come now to the central message of this book, and we'll answer some age-old questions. How does quantum physics relate to the Bible? Specifically, how does it relate to praise and worship from the believer to God? Can words and music move matter? How did Jesus operate above the laws of physics?

Music can change the world because it can change people.
– Bono

I'm indebted to Annette Capps for the following. In her book, *Quantum Faith,* she reveals several very helpful insights into quantum theory. The following is my paraphrase of some of the things she said.

> Jesus said, "If you would have faith as a mustard seed, you would say..." (Luke 17:6a).
>
> The mustard seed was the smallest of all seeds during Jesus' ministry on earth. If He were saying this today, He might say, "If you had faith as an atom or a subatomic particle, you would say..."
>
> Notice that He's very specific about our *saying* things. He instructed us to talk to things. The message here is, bigger things are made up of smaller things we can't see with the naked eye, but all things are built with these tiny, subatomic particles.
>
> Energy affects matter. Words and music frequencies are containers of energy.

They hold the frequencies (energy) of life or death (anti-life).

An interesting study has brought to light that subatomic particles behave differently if they are being observed. They also behave differently with each observer. Is it possible that these particles behave according to what the scientists *believe*? Sounds like faith! Could this explain why people have varied levels of success in life?

The things you desire are made up of atoms. They hear your words. They're sensitive to your beliefs and respond accordingly. After all, they're all created by words.

In Mark 11:14, Jesus spoke to the fig tree. "Let no one eat fruit of you ever again." That fig tree dried up from the subatomic level.

When He spoke to the wind and waves, they obeyed Him. He demonstrated this to teach His disciples that they could do this too.[2]

All matter is made up of atoms—you, your car, TV, children, the weather, computer, house, literally everything.

We are created in the image of God. That is, we are in the God class because we are speaking spirits. Like God, our words create. Once you start thinking in terms of quantum physics, verses like this one take on a deeper meaning: "Now faith is the substance of things hoped for, the evidence of things not seen," (Hebrews 11:1).

The Holy Spirit, who is the power behind the actual physical creation of the universe, said in Hebrews that faith has a tangible substance and it has evidence, which is hard copy provability. We also discover in the scriptures that faith is in two places, in the heart and in the mouth.

Faith is conceived in the heart, through mental pictures, goals, and dreams. It is released into the atmosphere by the mouth with words that say the same thing God has said in His Word.

That entire process is quantum physics in its most vivid demonstration.

The highest-level frequencies of *God* are his *words*. They are what created the universe. We can load them into our hearts and minds, and launch them out of our mouths into our lives and the lives of others. When we do, things will change.

When we speak and sing *toxic* sounds into the atmosphere around us, and into our own ears, we are causing a self-perpetuating harvest of defeat. (A common example of this is jokes about aging – "Having a senior moment," etc.) We find ourselves trapped in a never-ending cycle of failure. The tragedy is that we create the very thing that defeats us, and then blame it on someone else.

Our Creator gave us five physical senses to enable us to navigate in our physical world. When we attempt to use those physical senses to operate in the spiritual realm, we find ourselves frustrated because it can't produce the needed results. The world of the spirit operates in a higher and different dimension. It has different rules that govern it.

Spiritual Keys Unlock Natural Doors, Not the Other Way Around

Spiritual keys defy natural explanation. There is no mathematical explanation for a person planting a financial seed into the Kingdom of God and seeing it returned to them later, multiplied many times over. It just doesn't make natural sense.

And yet, God said, "Give, and it will be given to you: good measure, pressed down, shaken together, and running over will be put into your bosom. For with the same measure that you use, it will be measured back to you [again]," (Luke 6:38). That's a spiritual law. In everyday language it's saying, "If you use a teaspoon to measure your giving, that's what will come back to you. But if you use a shovel, you can expect increase to be shoveled back into your life."

Mark, chapter four, deals with *where* we sow our seed. If we're careful to sow into good fertile spiritual ground, we can be assured of a bumper crop at harvest time.

Likewise, the classic laws of physics regarding gravity say that if a 180-pound man steps onto the surface of a body of water, he will sink. When Jesus walked on water He must have known about a spiritual law that superseded the law of gravity.

Strange Quantum Behavior

What is it you desire? The bigger question is, "What are you choosing?" The possibilities for your life are unlimited!

Quantum physics is a realm where the known laws of physics (Newtonian physics) no longer apply. In classic (Newtonian) physics you can repeat experiments using the same formulas and get the answers and responses you expect. The experiments are repeatable. You can expect that this is the way things work. For instance, when Isaac Newton saw the apple fall from the tree to the ground, he discovered a natural law, gravity. You can experiment with gravity all you like and it will work every time. What goes up must come down! If you jump off the roof of your house, you will always go down, not up.

In the quantum subatomic arena, there are only possibilities and probabilities. Things don't work like you think they should. Nothing is there until you look and expect. All that exists is only an infinite number of possibilities. (Remember, Jesus said, "All things are possible to him that believeth," (Mark 9:23).)

Whereas gravity works whether anyone is present or not (a tree falls down, not up, even if no one observes it), subatomic particles are not there unless someone (an observer) looks for them. We can't really know what they are doing, or even if they exist, when we are not looking. It is possible that they "are not." 1 Corinthians 1:28 says that God has chosen the "things that are not to bring to naught things that are."

How can a thing not be? This scripture makes no sense at all until you bring it down to the atomic level. All things are made of atoms, which are made of subatomic particles. These particles are not really particles because they exist only in a state of possibilities until someone observes them, at which point they appear as a thing (particle).

When you hope for something, where does it exist? *Only in your mind and heart.* It "is not." It is only a possibility.

Through faith we understand the worlds were framed by the word of God, so that things which are seen were not made of things which do appear," (Hebrews 11:3). This is a statement that could have been made by a physicist!

What makes it appear? You, the observer, with faith that gives substance to your hopes and dreams.[3]

In view of this information, let's take a fresh look at John 20:19. "Then, the same day at evening, being the first *day* of the week, when the doors were shut where the disciples were assembled, for fear of the Jews, Jesus came and stood in the midst, and said to them, "Peace *be* with you."

It is very possible that Jesus transformed Himself into subatomic particles, smaller than the molecules and atoms in that closed door, passed through the door's materials, and reassembled Himself on the other side. The disciples had seen many miracles in the previous three years of traveling with Jesus, but I dare say that this one was way over the top.

The Law of Conservation of Matter states that matter (with no regard to particle size or location) can never be created or destroyed. It can only be changed and rearranged. Like atoms, energy cannot disappear, only relocate.

The particles of Jesus' body changed and rearranged themselves to pass through the solid surface. Then they rearranged themselves back to his former state.

How great is our God!

CHAPTER FOUR

THE SOUNDS
OF THE UNIVERSE

The song of the stars harmonizes with the rhythm of the trees clapping their hands in praise. The universe opens its voice making a heart cry of worship to its Creator.

The first two building blocks of the universe were sound and light. God said, "Light be..." and light appeared. Embedded within all that exists in our ever-expanding universe is the complete representation of divine frequencies – the imprint of the very first words and music, the Master Artist's sonic signature.

1 Corinthians 14:10 says it this way, "There are, it may be, so many kinds of voices in the world, and none of them is without signification" (KJV). Each voice in the entire cosmos, macro or micro, sounds a tone of disclosure and revelation, having a spiritual address embedded within. We could call this address the DNA of God, what physicists call the Higgs-Boson Particle or The God Particle.

From the BBC News Science and Environmental Department, Pallab Shnosh published an article on June 22, 2010 entitled "God particle signature is simulated as sound." The essence of this report is quite revealing.

Deep underground, 50 to 175 meters, near the French-Swiss border lies the massive Hadron Collider. It is a labyrinth of 17 miles of tunnels, magnets, sensors and sophisticated tracking equipment designed to look deep into the world of subatomic particles. As these particles collide with one another, there are unmistakable, trackable effects that occur.

The process of converting scientific data into sounds is called sonification. Scientists on the project have found that assigning sounds to the collisions—sonification—is the best way to convert the data measuring energy levels, particle behavior and more. The machine is designed to shed light on fundamental questions in physics.

The study was designed in hopes of giving physicists another way to analyze data. The team believes that human ears are well suited to catch the subtle changes that might indicate a new particle.

Richard Dobson, a composer involved with the project, says that he is "struck at how musical the products of collisions sound. We can hear clear structures in the sound, almost as if they had been composed. They seem to tell a little story all to themselves. They're so dynamic and shifting all the time, it does sound like a lot of the music that you hear in contemporary composition."

A Religious Experience

Archer Endrich says that, "those who have been involved in the project have felt something akin to a religious experience while listening to the sounds. You feel closer to the mystery of 'NATURE,' which I think a lot of scientists do when they get deep into these matters. It's so intriguing and there's so much mystery and so much to learn. The deeper you go, the more of a pattern you find and it's fascinating and uplifting."

Manmade religion is a box filled with
time-frozen frequencies, once living spiritual material that
was trapped, suffocated and fossilized.
– Len Mink

The Bible says this in Romans 1:20, "For since the creation of the world His invisible attributes are clearly seen, being understood by the things that are made, even His eternal power and Godhead, so that they are without excuse."

Psalm 140 in *The Living Bible* tells us:

> Praise the Lord, O heavens! Praise him from the skies! Praise him, all his angels, all the armies of heaven. Praise him, sun and moon and all you twinkling stars. Praise him, skies above. Praise him, vapors high above the clouds. Let everything he has made give praise to him. For he issued his command, and they came into being; he established them forever and forever. His orders will never be revoked.
>
> And praise him down here on earth, you creatures of the ocean depths. Let fire and hail, snow, rain, wind, and weather all obey. Let the mountains and hills, the fruit trees and cedars, the wild animals and cattle, the snakes and birds, the kings and all the people with their rulers and their judges, young men and maidens, old men and children—all praise the Lord together. For he alone is worthy. His glory is far greater than all of earth and heaven.

Creation Sings

The entire cosmos is emitting melodic frequencies, which we call songs. As we penetrate deeper into the outer regions of space and the inner frontiers of the subatomic world, there seems to be a nonstop stream of sounds arranged in an intelligent manner. Perhaps it is the echo of the original sonic download of creation. God has surrounded Himself with a vast and complex orchestra and choir of praise and worship, sounds so varied and complex as to defy the wildest imagination.

If all creation sings, that means there is a massive and varied cosmic saturation of sound going forth as a continuous praise to our God. It means that nature, every created thing, angels in Heaven, the subatomic world and literally *all* that was created are joining together in praise to God.

We've gleaned this from the Bible and sung about it for generations. Notice the lyrics to the famous hymn "This is My Father's World."

> This is my Father's world,
> And to my list'ning ears
> All nature sings, and round me rings
> The music of the spheres.
> This is my Father's world:
> I rest me in the thought
> Of rocks and trees, of skies and seas—
> His hand the wonders wrought.
>
> This is my Father's world:
> The birds their carols raise,
> The morning light, the lily white,
> Declare their Maker's praise.
> This is my Father's world:
> He shines in all that's fair;
> In the rustling grass I hear Him pass,
> He speaks to me everywhere.

The Gift of Choice

It's interesting to note that mankind, the apple of God's eye and the highest and best of His creative grandeur, has been given the highest of all gifts—choice.

God is love, and for love to be love, free will must be involved. We have a choice; we can sit down, bleeding in the ditches and blaming others for our misfortune. That is our right of choice. Or we can get out of the ditch of self-focus and take our place on the highway of life. We can use our gift of choice to move away from toxic self-pity and into the positive flow of faith and possibility.

*Many astrophysicists say they are coming face to face
with God in their pursuit of a deeper revelation of
mathematics. As they press in and pursue, many
have confessed that they have come into a place of
mathematical perfection, which can only be God!*
– Len Mink

U.S. veteran public servant Madeleine Albright said, "What people have the capacity to choose, they have the ability to change."[4]

American author, Jim Butcher put it this way, "God isn't about making good things happen to you. He's all about you making choices—exercising the gift of free will. God wants you to have good things and a good life, but He won't gift wrap them for you. You have to choose the actions that lead you to that life."

A great example of one making good choices is found in the letter written in March 1924 to the New York Symphony Orchestra by Helen Keller:

> **Dear Friends,**
>
> *I have the joy of being able to tell you that, though deaf and blind, I spent a glorious hour last night listening over the radio to Beethoven's Ninth Symphony. I do not mean to say that I heard the music in the sense that other people heard it; and I do not know whether I can make you understand how it was possible for me to derive pleasure from the symphony.*
>
> *It was a great surprise to myself. I had been reading in my magazine for the blind of the happiness that the radio was bringing to the sightless everywhere. I was delighted to know*

that the blind had gained a new source of enjoyment; but I did not dream that I could have any part of their joy.

Last night, when the family was listening to your wonderful rendering of the immortal symphony someone suggested that I put my hand on the receiver and see if I would get any of the vibrations. He unscrewed the cap, and I lightly touched the sensitive diaphragm.

What was my amazement to discover that I could feel, not only the vibration, but also the impassioned rhythm, the throb and the surge of the music! The intertwined and intermingling vibrations from different instruments enchanted me. I could actually distinguish the cornets, the roil of the drums, deep-toned violas and violins singing in exquisite unison. How the lovely speech of the violins flowed and plowed over the deepest tones of the other instruments! When the human voices leaped up thrilling from the surge of harmony, I recognized them instantly as voices more ecstatic, upcurving swift and flame-like, until my heart almost stood still.

The women's voices seemed an embodiment of all the angelic voices rushing in a harmonious flood of beautiful and inspiring sound. The great chorus throbbed against my fingers with poignant pause and flow. Then all the instruments and voices together burst forth an ocean of heavenly vibration and died away like winds when the atom is spent, ending in a delicate shower of sweet notes.

Of course this was not hearing, but I do know that the tones and harmonies conveyed to me moods of great beauty and majesty. I also sensed, or thought I did, the tender sounds of nature that sing into my hand swaying reeds and winds and the murmur of streams. I have never been so enraptured before by a multitude of tone vibrations.

As I listened, with darkness and melody, shadow and sound filling the room, I could not help remembering that the great composer who poured forth such a flood of sweetness into the world was deaf like myself. I marveled at the power of his quenchless spirit by which out of his pain he wrought such joy for others and there I sat, feeling with my hand the magnificent symphony which broke like a sea upon the silent shores of his soul and mine.[5]

Helen Keller experienced this same creative burst of tangibility even though it was limited to her touch. The musical vibrations and the frequencies she felt were converted into some of the most beautiful words ever uttered. How much more are we, with all our senses, capable of experiencing and sharing?

As mysterious as this may sound to the natural mind, part of the ministry of the Holy Spirit at creation was to take the words and frequencies of God's faith-filled declarations and make of them hard copy.

Take God's Word for instance. It carries within it everything needed to bring us to the revelations that will lead us to the right decisions and onward to glorious manifestations. The Bible, this collection of supernatural frequencies, is one with the Creator. It's very interesting that Jesus is called the Living Word. Not the Living Thought. Not the Living Idea. Not the Living Theory.

Jesus is the Word of God in human form. He said, "If you've seen me, you've seen the Father" (John 14:9). He also said, "I only do and say what I hear or see my Father do and say" (John 12:49, John 5:19).

God and everything that came forth from Him reverberates with the same frequencies of life, from the most distant galaxy to the tiny Higgs-Boson sub-atomic particle. It seems our loftiest and smartest goal in life should be to do whatever is necessary to "sympathetically vibrate" and flow with Life Himself.

Doing our own thing is a self-constructed prison. However, flowing with God on every level offers remarkable, non-expendable creativity, freedom, and rewards. You are God's hard copy, the pinnacle of His creation.

Understanding sound lays a foundation for developing a lifestyle of praise. Praise connects us in a supernatural way to an endless supply of divine frequencies, which are the means that God uses to convey His bountiful supply to us. This experience reminds me of the old Gospel song, "Turn Your Radio On," which urges listeners to tune in to a certain frequency. In the simplest terms, that's what we do with praise.

Praise should be the top priority of the human spirit, as it connects us to the heart and character of God. It duplicates each facet of the Divine Personality to us. This relationship is the love and grace of God pursuing us through a myriad of infinitely creative avenues, hunting us down to express His ultimate love. Praise connects us to the eternal.

The little black and white dot matrix found in early pictures of DNA looks like a piano keyboard. DNA may be our own personal musical score.

Praise connects us to the eternal. When you live a praise centered lifestyle, it creates domestic peace and minimizes psychological trauma, stress and anxiety. One cannot genuinely praise God and walk in unforgiveness at the same time.

He is also the source of our identity. In our search for significance, we often confuse identification and identity. Identification refers to the labels we wear. They tell the world, and ourselves, who we think we are. Identity is the essence of our core being. Confusing these two things is a recipe for personal disaster. Real identity can only come to us from God, our Maker.

In Scripture, there is much more emphasis on praise than there is on prayer, even though each is sound related. Biblical descriptions of the sounds of Heaven paint a vivid picture of worship and praise as the central focus of time and energy for all the inhabitants. This must be a fitting pattern on earth. Jesus said in the Lord's prayer, "On earth as it is in Heaven."

Praise is a mighty force in combating every enemy of the human journey, whether mental, physical, or spiritual. It's a well established fact that most doctor visits are directly or indirectly related to stress, often resulting from self-condemnation and worry. Worship is a cathartic, therapeutic activity providing a divinely designed pressure release valve. Stress-free people have a higher overall success rate in marriage, parenting, finances, health and their positive impact on others.

Speaking in nutritional terms, praise is at the top of the list of super foods. Developing praise as a high priority allows us to respond to life's problems from a position of strength. Otherwise, we react each day to unfolding problems.

This unbroken fellowship with God keeps our spiritual tanks full instead of letting them run on empty. There is an old saying that's true. One percent of your life is determined by what happens to you. The other 99 percent is determined by how you respond.

If we believe that life is a gift, we must realize that a response from us to the Giver is appropriate. This is a very back-and-forth flow of life, which is the essence of the Great Exchange that took place when our debt was paid by the love and grace of God through the sacrifice of Jesus.

A consistent, authentic life of praise is the highest expression of faith to a loving, beneficent and involved God. It connects us to a nonstop life of purpose, empowerment, and fulfillment. It leads to a life well lived.

CHAPTER FIVE

QUANTUM FAITH

We live in a voice-activated universe.

In the beginning, the Holy Spirit was brooding, hovering, fluttering over a surging, chaotic mess—waiting for words.

In the following scripture quotation from the Bible, I added the parenthesized words from the meanings of the original Hebrew root words. *This* is what the Holy Spirit was brooding over:

> In the beginning God created the heaven (*space above the physical earth) and the earth (to be firm, land, ground)*. And the earth was without form, *(wasteland, desolation on the surface, desert, worthless, confused empty place, without shape, nothing)*, and void *(to be empty, vacant, undistinguishable, ruin)*; and darkness *(misery, destruction, death, ignorance, sorrow, wickedness, hidden in darkness)* was upon the face *(forefront part, part that turns and presents its appearance to the onlooker) of the deep (abyss, surging mass of water and solid material [mud])*. And the Spirit of God moved *(intense energy, wind [sound] of a rational being)* upon the face of the waters (Genesis 1:1-2, KJV Emphasis mine).

God had an image in mind of how it should look. He downloaded that image into words. Then He spoke those image-laden words into that teeming, roiling chaos. The Holy Spirit was on site, waiting for words that would bring order, balance, productivity and beauty to the chaos.

When those divine frequencies were spoken by God, then and only then was there substance to inject into the chaos to bring order, creativity, and purpose.

Words are substance.

It took the substance of God's Words to change a chaotic mess into a beautiful jewel. It's widely believed that this creative miracle all happened at the same time.

God's spoken words are still creating worlds at the speed of light.

Things Obey Words

Material things were created by words. Therefore, it stands to reason that they would still respond to words. Learning that *things obey words* made a huge impact on my life.

In Genesis 2:7, according to the *Jewish Babylonian Aramaic* translation of the Bible called the *Targum* authored by a famous convert to Judaism named Onkelos, we learn that we were made in the image of God. We are "speaking spirits" in that we have a voice with which to speak things into existence.

In other words, we *are* spirits.

We *have* a soul, made up of a mind, will, emotions, and memory.

And we *live* in a body.

When Jesus came to earth, He put away His divine privileges and lived on earth as a man, just like us. He was a spirit, had a soul, and lived in a body.

Fig Tree Faith

It's interesting to watch how Jesus dealt with a fig tree and taught about faith.

For many months, He based his ministry out of the home of friends, siblings Mary, Martha and Lazarus. That location was in Bethany, about two miles east of Jerusalem on the southeast slope of the Mount of Olives. Look at how He spoke to a fig tree and how He compared it to the operation of faith.

> Now the next day, when they had come out from Bethany, He was hungry. And seeing from afar a fig tree having leaves, He went to see if perhaps He would find something on it. When He came to it, He found nothing but leaves, for it was not the season for figs. In response Jesus said to it, "Let no one eat fruit from you ever again."

In the original King James Version, it says in verse 14 that Jesus *answered* the fig tree. Very interesting.

And His disciples heard *it* (Mark 11:12-14).

The next morning, the disciples saw a shocking sight.

> Now in the morning, as they passed by, they saw the fig tree dried up from the roots. And Peter, remembering, said to Him, "Rabbi, look! The fig tree which You cursed has withered away." So Jesus answered and said to them, "Have faith in God. For assuredly, I say to you, whoever says to this mountain, 'Be removed and be cast into the sea,' and does not doubt in his heart, but believes that those things he says will be done, he will have whatever he says. Therefore I say to you, whatever things you ask when you pray, believe that you receive *them*, and you will have *them* (Mark 11:20-24).

Jesus didn't speak to the fig tree just to prove that He was the son of God. He demonstrated it to let His disciples know that they too could speak words of power to mountains in their lives—and the mountains would obey.

This was a twenty-four hour manifestation. However, words are seeds and they may take time to germinate and bear fruit. Also, many people don't have a harvest on their seeds because they keep digging them up to see if anything is happening.

Things all around you are responding to your words every day. Whether you're aware of it or not, you're giving substance to your world through your words.

All things respond to the vibration of energy. A microwave bombards water molecules with higher-frequency waves. The molecules get agitated and move at a higher frequency. This generates heat. Enough heat makes the water boil. The opposite is also true. Cool the water until the hydrogen and oxygen molecules that make up H20 slow down and the water will freeze.

Have you ever asked yourself what kind of energy you're producing? Do you introduce faith-energized, high-frequency words to your children, your finances, and your health? Or are you using low frequency negative words that freeze your circumstances into a constant series of crises?

Many people think that if they spoke positive, faith-filled words into a negative situation, they would be lying. But by *not* speaking them, they are putting the final authority into the hands of circumstances, rather than the frequencies of the Word of God.

Words created the problem; and words can fix it. Would you rather reinforce that which exists, or do you want to change it? What is it that you desire? The more appropriate question is what are you choosing? The possibilities for your life are unlimited.

I believe that when we worship God out of a pure heart
and sing forth the mathematically pure and perfect Word
of God, all that is spirit, all that is soul, and all that is flesh
will resonate and sympathetically vibrate to the frequency
of the Unbegun One, the Most High God.
– Len Mink

A good ole boy from the country visited his friend who lived in the city. He walked from the hot, humid outdoors into his friend's house. He expected it to be hot indoors, but it was pleasant and cool. When he asked how that had happened, his friend tried to explain air conditioning to him by walking over to the thermostat on the wall and setting it to a cooler temperature.

The country boy jumped up and headed out the door.

"Where are you going in such a hurry?" his friend asked.

"I'm going down to the hardware store to get me one of those thermostat things to nail to my wall."

A funny story, for sure, but it illustrates the fact that our mouth is our thermostat. The thermostat calls for a temperature change by signaling the unit outdoors to produce the desired temperature. Our mouths generate words with either creative or destructive frequencies. We place them into the physical and spiritual atmosphere, calling for those words to come to pass.

Do not imprison Christ in you. Let Him manifest
Himself, let him find vent through you.
– John G. Lake, Spiritual Hunger and Other Sermons

Faith Framed the World

Faith-filled words formed the world. Hebrews 11:3 goes on to say, "Through faith we understand that the worlds are framed by the word of God, so that things which are seen were not made of things which do appear." This verse sounds like it could have been written by a physicist! Of course, the Creator is the first and greatest physicist of all times.

What makes it appear? You, the observer, with faith that gives substance to your hopes and dreams.[3] Faith observes that which *is not* and gives it substance, so that it might appear and become visible.

The key to manifesting matter is to interact with that which *is not*, so that it becomes the thing you hoped for. Your expectations and beliefs—or what you observe—are of primary importance. If you observe and expect failure, sickness, or disaster, that's exactly what will manifest.

Which possibility becomes reality? It's totally up to you. Be wise in what you choose.

Because quantum theory works so differently than what we're used to, we don't have the language to describe it. Most people aren't very interested in quantum physics because they don't understand it. However, as we study these introductory principles, it all begins to sound familiar, like faith language. The things we've learned about faith and confession are scientific facts.

We Can Do Greater

Jesus said, "Most assuredly, I say to you, he who believes in Me, the works that I do he will do also; and greater *works* than these he will do, because I go to My Father." (John 14:12).

By comparing quantum physics with spiritual law, I want to present to you a different way of thinking. Understanding this is going to open a whole new avenue for faith that moves mountains.

Faith is an unseen energy force. It's not matter, but it creates matter and becomes substance or matter. Faith-energized words convert energy to matter. Words are the catalysts that turn the substance of faith into physical manifestation. Faith is the raw material from which everything is made.

Everything is connected. We have been programed in this negative world to sow the wrong kind of seed and then wonder what happened. Quantum physics brings us back to the reality that Jesus taught that all things are connected.

We determine our outcomes by the seeds we sow. Our words are seeds. God is not in Heaven sowing seeds and making choices for us. God made that clear in Deuteronomy 30:19, "I call heaven and earth as witnesses today against you, that I have set before you life and death, blessing and cursing; therefore choose life, that both you and your descendants may live."

Generational curses start and are perpetuated without a divine revelation of the power of our words. Our ancestors unwittingly signed for the package. They believed and they said that certain diseases run in the family.

God said, "Death and life are in the power of the tongue..." (Proverbs 18:21a).

Charles Capps said, "A thought unspoken dies unborn."

It is too easy to coast along with negative, limiting thoughts and beliefs. They bring fear and depression. They manifest in your life as hopelessness and an expectation of sickness, poverty, failure, and defeat. They make you feel stuck.

You can reprogram your beliefs by speaking energizing, life-giving words of power and singing songs filled with the frequencies and lyrics of life. Speak and sing only what agrees with who Christ says you are, and you can eliminate the old belief system that has dominated you.

There are 138 verses in the New Testament where we are told who we are in Christ. I've taken a few of those vital scriptures and transposed the wording into declarations that personalize and internalize the great power of these divinely inspired words.

Read them aloud in the first-person. They will give you spiritual nourishment to soar far above mere intellectual contact with these cosmic truths.

Words Filled With Life

- I am strong in the Lord and in the power of His might. I draw strength from Him, that strength which His boundless might provides (Ephesians 6:10).

- I am strengthened with all might according to His glorious power. I can do all things through Christ who strengthens me (Colossians 1:11, Philippians 4:13).

- The same spirit that raised Christ from the dead dwells in me and quickens my mortal body (Romans 8:11).

- The law of the spirit of life in Christ Jesus has made me free of the law of sin and death (Romans 8:2).

As you meditate on who you are in Christ, be prepared for Him to remind you on occasion. That happened to me in a grocery store. I walked through the first set of sliding doors, grabbed a basket, and went through the second set into the grocery store. The first thing I noticed was a bird flying around inside. Cathy and I had shopped there for years, and the manager, Linda, was a rough old gal to whom I'd witnessed many times. She walked up to me puffing on a cigarette. "I want to tell you something," she said. "I'm in the food business here. Do you see that bird flying around?"

"Yes, I noticed."

"Do you know what that bird can do to my store?"

"I can imagine. Have you considered calling a pest control company?"

"I was just going to phone them when I saw you come in. You've told me about Jesus so often that it's time to put up or shut up. If your God's real, get rid of that bird and I'll believe."

I walked through the store praying, looking around at the size of it. I wandered over to Produce and stood in front of a big display with a mirror behind it. I picked up a bunch of celery, and then looked in the mirror at the vast expanse of the store. Catching a bird in a store that size seemed impossible.

"Don't do that," the Lord warned. *"Look at the celery. Stand there and have faith."*

My back to the door, I stood in faith holding the celery, praying in the Spirit.

The bird flew over and landed on the celery in my hand!

I sang "Jesus Loves Me," in a soft voice.

The bird cocked its head to one side and to the other.

As I sang, he seemed to calm down.

"Put your thumb on his toes and walk him out of the store."

I put my thumb on his toenails and started walking. He didn't like that at all and pecked at my knuckle about 50 times.

"I'm trying to save your life," I said.

I walked past all the cashiers and the people in lines. Everyone was watching. Linda was cussing. "I've never seen any #@*&% like it!"

Once I reached the outer door, I released the bird. I turned back in time to see three cashiers cross themselves and two ladies shouting, "Glory to God!" in Spanish.

The whole store burst out in applause.

"Okay," I said when I stopped in front of Linda. "Do you believe?"

"Yes, I do! I wouldn't have ever believed if that hadn't happened!"

The bird and Linda both were saved!

CHAPTER SIX

THE GIFT OF SPEECH

Speech is one of the greatest gifts endowed upon humanity by our Creator. Yet, we're so inoculated with its use that sometimes we fail to see its wonder and power. This amazing ability is capable of endless development. People with fine-tuned gifts of spoken or musical words influence great swaths of humanity.

Even short, single phrases can lift people from despair to hope or from sickness to wholeness. It can lift us from a sense of loss to a joyful sense of purpose. Our entire existence is determined by words we hear and those we speak. Our very identity, our search for significance, our self-worth, and our level of influence on others are all determined by words.

Most of us are familiar with the phrase, "One word from God can change your life forever." God also uses *our* words to help heal others. The reverse is also true. Death, hopelessness, hatred, fear and everything that hell offers is conveyed by words.

Our speech is an indicator of our character.

The Bible puts it this way in Matthew 12:34-37:

> Brood of vipers! How can you, being evil, speak good things? For out of the abundance of the heart the mouth speaks. A good man out of the good treasure of his heart brings forth good things, and an evil man out of the evil treasure brings forth evil things. But I say to you that for every idle word men may speak, they will give account of it in the day of judgment. For by your words you will be justified, and by your words you will be condemned.

Jesus said that we would either be approved or condemned by *our words.*

The greatest power that we've been given, and the weightiest responsibility, is how we use our words. This is why the renewing of our minds is so vital to living in victory.

The Lord also said, "And do not be conformed to this world, but be transformed by the renewing of your mind, that you may prove what *is* that good and acceptable and perfect will of God," (Romans 12:2).

About words, the Bible said, "For assuredly, I say to you, whoever says to this mountain, 'Be removed and be cast into the sea,' and does not doubt in his heart, but believes that those things he says will be done, he will have whatever he says. Therefore I say to you, whatever things you ask when you pray, believe that you receive *them,* and you will have *them,*" (Mark 11:23-24).

A renewed mind is essential to renewed thinking. Renewed thinking is vital to launching life-filled words. You have to think right to talk right. This requires self-discipline. 2 Corinthians 10:5b "…bringing every thought into captivity to the obedience of Christ."

Having a mind being renewed each day by a consistent diet of God's Word is the only way to be certain that your moral compass is aligned with the heart of God. It's like the balance of power on the global scene today. Nuclear power, or any form of power, must be accompanied by a balanced moral component as well as checks and balances and cross-accountability. Rogue nations and bad actors want the power, but they lack the moral core necessary to prevent its misuse.

Weapons of Mass Destruction

In today's world, any use of weapons of mass destruction not only destroys those being attacked, but the attackers as well. It's the same scenario with our words. For all the good we can do with our words, we often fall into a negative, destructive pattern. Without thinking, we utter devastating frequencies from our vocal cannons. We don't realize that with the language of hatred and division we are condemning ourselves.

This is spelled out for us in the third chapter of James:

> My brethren, let not many of you become teachers, knowing that we shall receive a stricter judgment. For we all stumble in many things. If anyone does not stumble in word, he *is* a perfect man, able also to bridle the whole body. Indeed, we put bits in horses' mouths that they may obey us, and we turn their whole body. Look also at ships: although they are so large and are driven by fierce winds, they are turned by a very small rudder wherever the pilot desires. Even so the tongue is a little member and boasts great things. See how great a matter a little fire kindles! (James 3:1-6).

According to this passage, a perfect man is one who bridles his tongue. That means, of course, that Jesus didn't stumble in his words. He used His tongue to bridle His entire body. Since our call is to be like Him, the first thing we must learn to do is bridle our tongues.

Verse eight in that same chapter tells us that the tongue "is an unruly evil, full of deadly poison." James continues by telling us that we should never use our tongue to curse men who were made in God's image.

> Out of the same mouth proceed blessing and cursing. My brethren, these things ought not to be so. Does a spring send forth fresh *water* and bitter from the same opening? Can a fig tree, my brethren, bear olives, or a grapevine bear figs? Thus no spring yields both salt water and fresh (James 3:10-13).

*What we hear and how we process it has a far
greater impact on our daily living than we realize. From
the womb to the moment we die, we are surrounded by
sound, and what we hear can either energize or deplete our
nervous systems. It is no exaggeration to say that what
goes into our ears can harm or heal us.*
– Joshua Leeds, The Power of Sound

Even though his word pictures are simple and basic, there's no doubt what James is saying. Every word, even a short one, is a short song. Each has a beginning, a middle and an end. They each have a key, rhythm, tempo and volume. Every word has a measureable frequency. Not only is it vital to choose the right words to download into each situation, but also to deliver them with the correct tone or musical structure.

Anger has a tone—a jagged painful note.

Joy has a tone—an uplifting, affirming and healing note.

According to the first chapter of Genesis, the original, primary mission of words was to bring order to chaos. Read how it's explained in Hebrews 1:1-3:

> God, who at various times and in various ways spoke in time past to the fathers by the prophets, has in these last days spoken to us by *His* Son, whom He has appointed heir of all things, through whom also He made the worlds; who being the brightness of *His* glory and the express image of His person, and upholding all things by the word of His power, when

He had by Himself purged our sins, sat down at the right hand of the Majesty on high.

Words were the original technology used by God. Every large and small fragment of our universe is made up of words spoken by God into the chaos. Words loaded with the DNA, the blueprint of God's plan, are seeds planted by the Almighty to generate the life of God everywhere—forever.

Most people don't realize the power of the words they have broadcast into the atmosphere of their lives. They watch as good or bad things happen and don't realize that they're the prophets of their own lives.

A year from now, you may wish
that you had started today.
– Karen Lamb

People enjoy the good things in life without giving them much thought, but bad things can become real stumbling blocks. Not knowing how to fix negative problems, people languish in dark, uncertain places. The person becomes a blame expert, carrying deeply embedded guilt and rejection. In time, they act out as an abuser on some level.

The reason there seems to be no way out is that they've never been made aware of the most foundational reason for the problems—their words. Words are the audio signature of an internal belief system.

Luke said it this way, "The good person out of the good treasure of the heart produces good, and the evil person out of evil treasure produces evil; for it is out of the abundance of the heart that the mouth speaks" (Luke 6:45 NRSV).

In Proverbs 4:23 we see that we're to "Keep your heart with all vigilance for from it flow the springs of life" (NRSV).

Proverbs 10:11 warns that, "The mouth of the righteous is a fountain of life, but the mouth of the wicked conceals violence" (NRSV).

These verses make it clear that the way to change your world is to change your words.

The best way to change your words from toxic to healthy is to change your heart, which is your spirit. You do that by making the things that are important to God, important to you. For instance, let His perspective on life become your belief system. Instead of a never-ending stream of natural thinking, renew your mind with what God's Word says.

Joining Forces with Heaven

The primary way that we join forces with Heaven, is by saying what Heaven says about everything. We set our life-navigating coordinates by the ultimate standard—God's Word.

Who do you say God is? It's much like speaking an address into the navigational app on your cell phone. Your voice will launch a search for the actual location that exists, and it will lead you there. The whole world is voice activated. When words are spoken, all the forces of the universe go into action to bring them to pass.

The thing God wants to know is what you say about Him. Are you speaking the frequencies of Heaven? Are you speaking the words of faith?

For instance, if you want divine protection, it's offered in Psalm 91. But this promise comes with conditions about what you must say.

> He who dwells in the secret place of the Most High shall abide under the shadow of the Almighty.
>
> I will *say* of the LORD, "*He is* my refuge and my fortress;

My God, in Him I will trust," (Psalm 91: -2, emphasis mine).

The second criterion we find in Psalm 91 is what God says in verse nine. Have you made the Lord your refuge and your dwelling place?

Because you have made the LORD, *who is* my refuge,

Even the Most High, your dwelling place,

No evil shall befall you,

Nor shall any plague come near your dwelling;

For He shall give His angels charge over you,

To keep you in all your ways, (v 9-11)

The third thing God wants to know is if you've set your love on Him. It's the same question that Jesus asked Peter, "Do you love me?"

"*Because he has set his love upon Me*, therefore I will deliver him;

I will set him on high, because he has known My name.

He shall call upon Me, and I will answer him;

I *will be* with him in trouble;

I will deliver him and honor him.

With long life I will satisfy him,

And show him My salvation," (v 14-16).

In both military and civilian mountain climbing, one way to scale a steep cliff is to throw a rope, with a grappling hook attached, to a point above you. As it grabs, you use it to pull yourself up. Likewise, speaking words of divine frequencies pulls you up to a higher level of life in Christ.

Words are our ladder of ascent into the presence of God. Words are also used to bring down that which we seek into our present need. That ladder is Jesus Himself, the Living Word. As we speak, sing, think and focus on Him and His promises, they will manifest.

Trust me, I have personal experience doing this. Something that helped me turn my mouth around was to remind myself each time I was about to speak, "Everything you say comes to pass—everything!" That should help each of us value the content and potential effect our words will have on ourselves and others.

There is a time-tested old saying: "Words have a life of their own. Think before you speak!" Don't copy the behavior and customs of the world. Let God transform you into a new person by changing the way you think—and speak. Then you'll learn to know God's will for your life, which according to Romans 12:2 is good and pleasing and perfect (NLT).

I want you to notice something in Mark 11:23. Note that believing in the heart is mentioned once. Speaking with the mouth is mentioned three times. You can have whatever you say.

"For assuredly, I say to you, whoever *says* to this mountain, 'Be removed and be cast into the sea,' and does not doubt in his heart, but believes that those things he *says* will be done, he will have whatever he *says*," (emphasis mine).

Most people pride themselves on being realists who "just tell it like it is." There is overwhelming evidence in Scripture that we shouldn't tell it like it is. We should tell it like God says it is to be.

CHAPTER SEVEN

THE TOWER OF BABEL AND THE POWER OF UNITY

South Africa's beauty was legendary, from the highest peak of Mafadi Mountain soaring at 11,320 feet, to verdant green valleys dotted with vineyards. The wildlife varied from penguins on the coastlines of the Atlantic and Indian Oceans, to the most stunning collection of wildlife seen in the world.

Although I'd seen those sights on my many trips to South Africa, that wasn't what I'd come to explore this time. I was far beneath the surface of the earth in a gold mine. I'd often been among the Zulu, Xhosa, Swati, Sotho, Basotho and Ndebele people, but I heard none of those languages in the mine. For reasons of safety and unity, each employee had to learn a common mining language called *Fanagalo*.

The language was unfamiliar to me. It sounded like a linguistic first cousin to Zulu, with English and a little Afrikaans thrown in. This was the only pidgin or simplified language recognized as being created from indigenous languages. It hadn't been colonized or traded. It was very interesting to my musical ear.

Having created this hybrid method of communication, where everyone in the mine spoke the same language, made the Tower of Babel even more poignant to me.

According to Genesis 11, the people of the earth spoke the same language. That could be taken literally or taken to mean that they were all unified in purpose. In either case, they had no trouble communicating with each other, and they were in sync with one another as a society.

As the story unfolds, we find the Babylonians building a high tower to reach Heaven in order to make a name for themselves. Their purpose was to follow the example of Lucifer— build a tower to Heaven and take over. God chose a clever scheme to stop their plan.

Notice as we visit this scene that sounds, words, frequencies, and most likely music were all involved in God's answer to their plot against Heaven. In Genesis 11:6, God said, "They are all speaking the same language and nothing they plan to do can be withheld from them."

In the following verse, He said, "Let's go down there and confound their language so that it will be impossible for them to communicate with one another or understand what's being said." God said, "Let *us* go down…" Since this means that more than one went down, it's possible that angels were involved in facilitating this sonic crash.

The frequency-bomb God dropped on the builders befuddled both their speaking and hearing so that it was incoherent. Thus, it became impossible for them to continue constructing the tower.

There was an interesting fact mentioned in verse four. They were afraid of being scattered around the earth, which is what God did in response to their plan. He confused their language and scattered them across the face of the earth. In other words, they knew that what they were doing was wrong. Yet, they purposed to defy God and attempt to take control.

Notice that the tower was made of bricks. They had one common language and identical bricks to build with instead of using stones. This is the core of the Babylonian system—pure socialism, everyone equal, no one rewarded for exceptional achievement and all things in common. All of it was enforced by huge government with one unified language. Since no two stones were alike, they used bricks and huddled in a closed city to assert control over all the inhabitants.

As Christians, in 1 Peter 2:5, the Bible calls us *lively stones*. We're all different sizes, shapes, colors and unique abilities. We're hewn from the Chief Cornerstone Himself. He is the Stone that the builders rejected. No two of us are alike, yet our commonality in Christ brings unity while allowing diversity in our corporate strength.

Christian believers aren't bricks!

In Him, we are being constructed into a living temple to become a holy priesthood. We offer spiritual sacrifices acceptable to God through Jesus Christ.

Connected to Supply

We have God-given gifts of individual and corporate exceptionalism. As an example, the United States of America decided at its inception to build a country and a people centered in Judeo-Christian ethics and theology. America came about because people wanted to escape tyranny and religious oppression. With that choice, the possibility of God's blessings became limitless. History stands as an irrefutable witness to that fact.

Just as supernatural is the fact that wherever we are in the world, no matter the government or conditions, believing Christians can enjoy indescribable peace, strength, favor, joy, and provision. Along with that, a sense of identity and purpose. We're connected to the supply available through our citizenship. We're not limited to the inadequacies of our surroundings. By faith, we reach into the fullness of the spirit realm and pull down what God has provided for here and now.

Music has the power to create a
universe or to destroy a civilization.
– Katherine Neville, The Eight

As we've learned, the language of faith is very similar to quantum terminology. You may recall that Hebrews 11:1 says, "Now faith is the substance of things hoped for, the evidence of things not seen." That's quantum talk.

So is Hebrews 11:3, "Through faith we understand the worlds were framed by the word of God, so that things which are seen were not made of things which do appear."

The *World English Bible* says it this way, "By faith, we understand that the universe has been framed by the word of God, so that what is seen has not been made out of things which are visible."

Even though the unity of language was used against the plans of God in Babylon, the unity of language principle works anywhere. As we choose to speak God's frequencies into our own individual world, we get into verbal lockstep and unity with God and one another.

When this happens, the words of Genesis 11:6 come alive to us. Only this time, it is on the positive side of things. "And the LORD said, Behold, the people is one, and they have all one language [they are all saying the same thing]; and this they begin to do: now nothing will be restrained from them, which they have imagined to do."

Dr. Andrew George is a professor in the Department of Languages and Cultures of the Near and Middle East, School of Oriental and African Studies at the University of London. Dr. George discovered an ancient tablet that provides the first image of the Tower of Babel. Interpreting the text, Dr. George found its account of the tower's construction was identical to the biblical story. Most scholars believe that Nimrod ruled the land when the construction began. Nebuchadnezzar II ruled during a season when repairs were being done on the structure.

Go back in time to the Garden of Eden. When Adam disobeyed God's edict, it stopped the flow of blessing and fellowship with God. Yet God began His plan of bringing mankind back to Himself. He inspired words to be spoken into the earth by prophets, establishing all that Jesus was to be.

Everything needed for the plan of salvation for mankind was in place. The words were spoken. The stage was set for Messiah to make His entrance.

When we embrace God's plan of redemption, it's all done with words. "That if thou shalt confess with thy mouth the Lord Jesus, and shalt believe in thine heart that God has raised Him from the dead, thou shalt be saved. For with the heart man believeth unto righteousness; and with the mouth confession is made unto salvation" (Romans 10:9-10, KJV).

"For God so loved the world, that he gave his only begotten Son, that whosoever believeth in him should not perish, but have everlasting life" (John 3:16).

Words—those sounds which communicate meaning—are containers that carry either positive or negative frequencies into the hearts and minds of those listening.

The Right to Remain Silent

The entertainment industry's fixation on police dramas has demonstrated the power of words to change lives. We can probably all recite the Miranda rights, which could be spoken to every person on earth. "You have the right to remain silent. Anything you say can and will be used against you..."

Spoken words can be translated from one language
to another, any language spoken around the world.
No such possibility exists with music.
– Author Unknown

What does that mean for you and me today? That we should say what God says about our situations. We are to find promises in God's Word that cover our circumstances and line up with our needs. We are to pray and speak them. We are to sing them, write them and listen to them. We are to look at them over and over until those words, declared in faith, change the landscape of our lives.

Think about this: God placed a demand on Adam's hidden abilities by having him name all the animals. Words generated by Adam went forth into the animals, not just as labels, but as destinies. His words programmed their future and their function on earth.

If you don't put a demand on your potential, you'll die with it unrealized.

Just about everything Jesus did, He did with words.

Not only do most people not know we're to speak what God says, few understand the way God designed man to function. Your own words of faith teach your heart to believe. Here it is in four simple steps.

Step 1: Imagine it. Get an image of it down on the inside of you.

Step 2: Believe it. Don't just admit that it's possible, but be convinced deep down that it's yours.

Step 3: Say it. Once the image is formed and your belief is in place, continue to feed the image with your words.

Step 4: Have it. Stand firm on the words that were declared, and don't say anything contrary to your original words. Let the power of the frequencies of your declaration work freely in an atmosphere of faith and thanksgiving.

With that having been established, I want to share excerpts from a very impressive article. Written by Elizabeth Youmans, the name of the article is "What Difference Do Words Make?" It was published at Darrow Miller and Friends on November 14, 2018. It is succinct and focused information on the power of words to shape our culture. After reading this information, I pray you will sense the wakeup call contained here and use your words to choose life.

The Bible teaches us that words are spirit. Jesus Christ, the Incarnate Word, said, "My words are spirit and they are life" (John 6:63). Words are the very substance or building blocks of ideas, and ideas have consequences! Word meanings inspire ideas that direct the pathway of our thinking and reasoning which lead to choices and consequences! Mastering and communicating with a biblical vocabulary is a high priority for Christian leaders, teachers, and parents.

It is a grievous fact that even many theological seminaries and Bible colleges teach from a secular philosophy of education. There may be pockets within the curriculum that are biblical, however, the worldview of most instructors, certainly the textbooks that they use, and the methods they employ to teach are progressive and humanistic. Students do not graduate with a renewed mind or supernatural faith.

By and large, our colleges and universities worldwide espouse humanism, as well. Professors seek acceptance by other scholars based on common-ground presuppositions. These presuppositions are always humanistic, for they assert the existence of authoritative standards apart from God and apart from a confession of supernatural faith. This is a declaration of the existence of an independent truth higher than that of the Bible. Therefore, most Christians have a dualistic mindset. They separate their secular life from their spiritual life. Sunday is God's day and Monday through Saturday they spend thinking the world's way, solving problems the world's way, doing business the world's way, and teaching and learning the world's way.

The Bible has profound things to teach us, but many believers have no idea about what is said in Scripture as it relates to academia. Western civilization has a history of having taught the revelation of the Bible and having taught students how to reason with the revelation of God's Word. This affected thought, vocabulary usage, and literature. This has been lost today in Christian education. Few are able to think

"Christianly," articulate and defend a Christian worldview in the marketplace or persuade others to believe it! While many pursue materialistic goals in education, the enemy has subtly stolen our Christian educational heritage. Our vocabulary has been stripped of biblical imagery and ideals. We have lost the ideals of truth and beauty in our thought life and speech, and our reasoning has become secular. Allan Bloom's book (1988), *The Closing of the American Mind*, began with this disturbing statement: "There is one thing a professor can be absolutely certain of: almost every student entering the university believes, or says he believes, that truth is relative." With the truth and beauty of God's Word removed from the heart of our educational system, Americans are losing the war!

Today the enemy has lured our children away from enjoying the written word through the overuse of the visual image. Think of the hours a day that we Americans and our children sit passively watching visual images in movies, television programs, cartoons, videos, computers, the internet, video games, and computer courses. The written word has been abandoned for the visual image. Scientists now find that the brain is developing differently physiologically! How has the emphasis on the visual image rather than the written word impacted the ability of this generation to clothe ideas with words and effectively articulate thoughts? God obviously values the written and the spoken word.

CHAPTER EIGHT

GOD IN THE WATER

Dr. Masaru Emoto conducted an amazing experiment which he chronicled in the book *Hidden Messages in the Water.* In his experiment, Dr. Emoto took pure water, placed .500 cc in each of 50 petri dishes and froze them at -25°C (-13°F) for three hours. He then placed them in a refrigerator at -5°C (23°F) with a microscope attached to a camera.

He took photographs of water drops that were kept in a sound-proof atmosphere to create a baseline for comparisons. Repeating the exact same scientific setup, Dr. Emoto then spoke words of love and thanksgiving over the water. It formed amazing, spectacular crystalline designs.

Next, he took photographs of water from a nearby polluted lake. The pictures showed bizarre, malformed crystals. After speaking words of blessing and peace over the same toxic water, beautiful crystals formed. If words and sounds of love, blessing, honor, forgiveness, and peace can do that for the water in this experiment, imagine what they could do for us. Our bodies are 70 percent water.

Dr. Emoto then printed blessings and taped them facing inward onto bottles of pure water, leaving them there overnight. He did the same with negative words, taping them onto bottles. The following morning, the same microphotography process was conducted. Believe it or not, they had the same amazing results as with spoken words.

And we wonder why things just turn out negative and toxic, never connecting our words, thoughts or music to our present living conditions.

Dr. Emoto spoke, sang and wrote in his native language, Japanese, using his personal dialect and accent. While the Hebrew language seems to possess the perfect balance of divine frequencies, any language can carry destructive or constructive frequencies embedded within.

God has given us the great gift of choice. We can choose to flow in sympathetic harmony with God's divine frequencies and enjoy a life filled with blessings. Or we can choose to conduct our lives in a perpendicular direction, colliding at oblique angles with God's spiritual principles, reaping negative consequences.

Sound is everywhere, all the time, touching everything. Sound fills up earth space, outer space and inner quantum space. It networks, connects, and weaves all things together. It communicates, comforts, heals, and has the power to affect change in everything it touches. Sound is the audio track that accompanies all the video of life, as infinite as the very voice of God. It interprets what we see and gives meaning to life, helping us respond correctly to every stimulus.

Sound can bring order and harmony, or it can promote the wrong combinations of people, events and responses. It does this by creating an out of focus interpretation of ourselves and others. Many young lives have been stunted, damaged and sent down the wrong road because of toxic, death-filled words contained in songs or films. These words have been spoken to them and around them, especially during formative, preverbal years.

Many people have hardships and immense challenges. It's those who heard words of love, faith, and optimism who rise above the negative baseline of their beginnings. Success levels can always be traced back to words—those we hear or those that we say. What we hear from outside sources is vitally important, but what we hear ourselves say is even more vital.

It seems that life is roughly 50 percent visual and 50 percent sound. Sometimes sound overpowers the visual; other times it's vice versa. We often get inoculated to the presence of the 800-pound sonic gorilla in the room, being bombarded with sound and images.

Two Fundamental Building Blocks

Whether you believe the Big Bang Theory or the biblical account of creation, the first two fundamental building blocks of the universe were sound and light. Following the account found in Scripture, sound created light and everything thereafter. Genesis 1:3 says, "And God said, let there be light and there was light. The *Message Bible* reads, "God spoke 'light' and light appeared."

As I've mentioned before, according to Genesis 1:14-18, light came into being before God created the sun, moon, planets, or solar system. Sound was the creating force loosed by God to bring all of creation to pass, both those things we've discovered and those which will be discovered in the future. Those first sounds out of the mouth of the Creator set His pattern for man and the universe. All that exists in our ever-expanding universe has embedded within it the complete representation of those original divine frequencies.

All created matter contains the imprint of those first sounds, the Master Artist's sonic signature. As you know by now, it's very possible that melody accompanied God's "Let there be…"

Opinions in both the theological and the scientific communities suggest that God *sang* the worlds into existence. The theological perspective seems to have peremptory dominance in creation discussions, because science is the discipline of discovering what already exists, not how it got there.

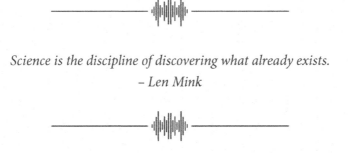

Science is the discipline of discovering what already exists.
– Len Mink

Modern quantum theories suggest that sound is at the very inner core of all creation, down to the most minute subatomic particle. Thus, making sound the very fabric of the universe.

Life on every level is replete with an almost infinite representation of sound. Sound has a limitless array of expressions and applications. It is everywhere we go, a huge part of everyday life. Sound is vital in interpreting what we see and in determining our position in the world around us. Every savvy retailer understands the selling power of sound, especially music. Most products advertised for sale have some sort of jingle, sound effect, or musical hook attached to them.

The human mind remembers information transported in song more than the spoken word. It's very difficult to become immune to music's persuasive power. Remember how much easier it was in school to learn the alphabet with the "ABC" song?

Sound is used in education, science, healing, psychotherapy, research, manufacturing, medicine, sports, religion, the military, and virtually every area of life on the planet.

The Physics of it All

The most general definition of sound is the "audible part of a transmitted signal." We may only feel the low-frequency pressure hitting our body, while not hearing the sound with our ears. In canine combat and law enforcement training, handlers are given a very high frequency whistle to get the dogs' attention or to give commands. The dogs can hear this frequency, but humans cannot.

The Long-Range Acoustic Device (LRAD) is a sound cannon developed by the military. This weapon, along with ultrasonic weapons, uses sound to injure, disorient, incapacitate, or kill an opponent. Some of these new weapons have been described as sonic bullets, sonic grenades, sonic mines, or sonic cannons. Some make a focused beam of sound or ultrasound, and some make a wide field of sound.

These devices are used in many ways, from repelling pirates at sea to dispersing riot crowds. For instance, following the G20 Summit in Pittsburg on September 25, 2009, police used pepper gas and an acoustic device that emitted an ear-splitting noise to send protestors fleeing for cover. There are very low-frequency sound devices that can shake a building apart or cause deep tissue damage in humans.

During World War II, the Korean War and the Vietnamese War, all sides of the conflict learned the power of transmitting high volume irritating sounds through large speakers toward their enemies. It's interesting to note that, in addition to irritating mechanical sounds, the sounds transmitted were edgy, raw, dissonant rock and roll songs. These seemed to disrupt the hearers' ability to focus or think clearly.

This technique was especially effective against ground troops, who were forced to hold their position, unable to escape the audio torture. This kind of acoustic force was used during interrogations to deny the enemy prisoners sleep, and to break down their defenses.

All created matter emits frequencies on a myriad of levels. These are most likely an eternally energized echo imprint of the divine frequencies which created it. It's as though every particle of the universe has a sound track that it plays over and over again.

Job 38:7 describes, "When the morning stars sang together and all of the sons of God shouted together." The original Hebrew root words in this scripture mean "to creak or emit a stridulous sound; to shout for joy and triumph."

In this age of the internet, we can hear stellar music with the push of a computer key. This works through sonifcation, or the conversion of scientific data into sound.

Think of it this way: the universe is not a silent film. It moves and wobbles, groans and pulses, expanding at the speed of light and faster. Scientists are discovering these three stunning realities:

1. The universe had a definite beginning (Stephen Hawking).

2. The universe is just right for life.

3. DNA coding reveals intelligence

The chances of the universe, in all its mathematical perfection and order, resulting from a giant, random cosmic explosion (Big Bang Theory) is akin to an unabridged dictionary resulting from an explosion in a print shop.

The late, famed cosmologist and theoretical physicist Stephen Hawking wrote, "If the rate of expansion one second after the big bang had been smaller by even one part in a hundred thousand million million, the universe would have re-collapsed before it reached its present size."[6]

Dr. Hawking, a pioneer of the black-hole theory in the 1970s, conceded that information can escape from black holes after all. [7] Not long before his death, Dr. Hawking, speaking to the international weekly journal of science *Nature* said, "There are no black holes. The notion of an event horizon from which nothing can escape is incompatible with quantum theory. There is no escape from a black hole in classical theory, but quantum theory enables energy and information to escape."

This is significant because more than 40 years ago, Dr. Hawking led the way in black hole discovery and research. Much to his credit, he admitted there is much more to be learned. What a brilliant mind. I believe that somewhere along his earthly journey he invited the Maker into his heart.

There lies within my quote, "Science is the discipline of discovering what already exists," a linear journey of discovery. Passing through unchartered frontiers always leads us to yet another boundary waiting to be crossed and new revelations to be held dear and utilized.

The Gospel is No Myth

Albert Einstein, in the last few years of his life, said in an interview with George Sylvester, "No one can read the Gospels without feeling the actual presence of Jesus. His personality pulsates in every word. No myth is filled with such life."[8]

Many people live their lives according to 2 Timothy 3:7, "ever learning and never able to come to the knowledge of the truth." Thankfully, faith connects us to the benefits of knowing the end results from the beginning.

Paul said in Philippians 3:14, "I press toward the mark for the prize of the high calling of God in Christ Jesus." Paul suggests that life is like a connect-the-dots puzzle. We make a maximum sustained effort to walk by faith from dot to dot, knowing that each dot will lead us to the completed picture. Unlike natural progression, we can walk through the process of life enjoying the benefits of the finished work of Christ, right from the beginning of the journey.

Abraham is our father in the presence of God in whom he believed. Romans 4:17 says, "I have made you the father of many nations," (NET). This is the same God who makes the dead alive and summons the things that do not yet exist as though they already do.

This is a supernatural work of grace and faith. Grace, God's unmerited favor, gave us faith to unlock to us the benefits of the finished process. This is because Jesus had already made it available to us for the asking and receiving. In Revelation 22:17b we're told, "Whosoever will, … let him take the water of life freely." It could be said, "Grace makes it and faith takes it."

As hard as it might be to comprehend, sound has everything to do with unleashing the benefits of salvation into our lives. So many scriptures make it clear that what we believe in our hearts will be spoken out of our mouths. This follows the example God set at creation. We, like God, are triune beings: we *are* spirits; we *have* souls; and we *live* in earth suits called bodies.

In other words, God is a Spirit. John 4:24 says, "God is a Spirit: and they that worship him must worship him in spirit and in truth."

Unlike humans, God has no physical body. This is the reason we can't see him. "Now faith is the substance of things hoped for, the evidence of things not seen," (Hebrews 11:1).

Perhaps *The Voice* translation explains it best. "Faith is the assurance of things you have hoped for, the absolute conviction that there are realities you've never seen. It was by faith that our forbearers were approved. Through faith we understand that the universe was created by the word of God; everything we now see was fashioned from that which is invisible."

It doesn't take a rocket scientist to realize that people speak out what's in their hearts. These words, broadcast into our future, determine what lies before us as we enter our tomorrows. The natural tendency is to say, "I'll believe it when I see it." This takes no faith at all. Faith says of itself, "Faith is being sure of what we hope for and certain of what we do not see."

"For by faith we understand that the worlds were fashioned by the word of God, and those things that are seen came into being out of those things which are unseen," (Hebrew 11:3, Aramaic Bible).

While we can't see God with our physical senses and faith seems to contradict the laws of scientific logic, many people are quick to assume that He doesn't exist. However, our God doesn't jump through scientific hoops. He has always been in existence. Science admits that there is a cause behind everything in existence. They are 100 percent correct about that.

The micro universe is proving to be vast as ongoing research peels away layers of inner space possibilities. Every facet of these worlds is filled with countless expressions of sound, once again demanding we focus on its amazing importance.

The more we understand about the power and purpose of sound, the more we can benefit from its riches. Only humans, gifted with choice, can create or destroy with the mighty power of sound.

CHAPTER NINE

HOW SOUND SHAPED YOUR BRAIN

Have you ever wondered how your brain was shaped? Some people do wonder, and they're called acoustic biologists. They study sounds made by living creatures, both human and animal. This study led to the discovery that humans can't hear many of the sounds that elephants make.

The following article by Bill McQuay and Christopher Joyce entitled "How Sound Shaped the Evolution of Your Brain" was published on *NPR* on September 10, 2015. I've also included some of *Morning Edition's* summer series, "Close Listening: Decoding Nature Through Sound."

Acoustic biologists who have learned to tune their ears to the sounds of life know there's a lot more to animal communication than just, "Hey, here I am!" or "I need a mate."

From insects to elephants to people, we all use sound to function and converse in social groups — especially when the environment is dark, or underwater or heavily forested.

"We think that we really know what's going on out there," says a Dartmouth College biologist, who studies crickets. But there's a cacophony all around us, she says, that's full of information still to be deciphered. "We're getting this tiny slice of all of the sound in the world."

Recently scientists have pushed the field of bioacoustics even further, to record whole environments, not just the animals that live there. Some call this "acoustic ecology" — listening to the rain, streams, wind through the trees. A deciduous forest sounds different from a pine forest, for example, and that soundscape changes seasonally.

Neuroscientist Seth Horowitz, author of the book *The Universal Sense: How Hearing Shapes the Mind*, is especially interested in the ways all these sounds, which are essentially vibrations, have shaped the evolution of the human brain.

"Vibration sensitivity is found in even the most primitive life forms," Horowitz says — even bacteria. "It's so critical to your environment, knowing that something else is moving near you, whether it's a predator or it's food. Everywhere you go, there is vibration and it tells you something."

And hearing is special among senses, Horowitz says. Sound can travel a long way. It will propagate through anything — the ground, water. It works at night, goes around corners. "Sounds give you sensory input that is not limited by field of vision."

The Brain's Auditory Circuits

Given how well sound reflects what's going on around us, the brains of vertebrates — including humans — evolved to be exquisitely sensitive to it.

"You hear anywhere from 20 to 100 times faster than you see," Horowitz says, "so that everything that you perceive with your ears is coloring every other perception you have, and every conscious thought you have." Sound, he says, "gets in so fast that it modifies all the other input and sets the stage for it."

It can do that because the brain's auditory circuitry is less widely distributed than the visual system. The circuitry for vision "makes the map of the New York subway look simple," says Horowitz, whereas sound signals don't have as far to travel in the brain.

And sound gets routed quickly to parts of the brain that deal with very basic functions — "precortical areas," Horowitz says — that are not part of the wiring for conscious thinking. These are places where emotions are generated.

"We're emotional creatures," Horowitz says, "and emotions are evolutionary 'fast responses' — things you don't have to think about."

That speediness pays dividends in the survival department: "You hear a loud sound?" he says. "Get ready to run from it." Emotions are rapid delivery systems in the brain, and sound drives emotions.

So sound hits you in the gut. But sound is also rich with patterns that carry information.

"The brain is really a wet, sloppy drum machine," Horowitz says. "It's desperately seeking rhythms." Not only rhythm, but patterns in pitch too, that have a mathematical regularity that captures the brain's attention.

The sound of a familiar voice, for example, has its own set of rhythms and pitches. So do particular sounds in nature: birds, insects, rain. The Bayaka people, who live in the rain forest of Central Africa, incorporate the syncopation of falling rain into their music.[9]

Sounds that alarm us don't have those patterns. Consider what Horowitz calls "the sound everybody hates."[10] In the screech of a fingernail scraping a blackboard, the familiar rhythmic and tonal patterns there are broken — the sound is ragged, as in a scream.

Sound gets in your head and stays there. When the brain processes sound, it actually resonates with it, like a tuning fork that's been struck. You can hear the brain's resonance if you have the right equipment.

"If you play a sound to a frog, [and] drop an electrode into their auditory nerve, you will hear the sound that the frog is hearing," Horowitz says, "because it is so absolutely represented — a change in frequency or pitch will be represented in how the nerves fire."

And even *without* an introduced sound, the working brain makes its own sound continuously, Horowitz says. He calls it a "neuronal symphony."[11]

"It sort of sounds like a well-tuned, old-school radio noise or crackling sound," he says. "You start to hear tonality; and you start hearing little songs."

Horowitz can sometimes tell what part of a frog's brain he's tapping into with his electrode by its sound (a process that doesn't harm the frog, he says).

He's listened to just about anything you can hear on Earth, and has started thinking about sound that's unearthly.[12]

The Difference is Speech

This scientific research is nothing short of fascinating. One big difference between us and the rest of the animal kingdom is speech. The speech center in the human brain is designed to exercise dominion over the entire central nervous system. Spoken words command the entire being to respond according to the frequencies of the words spoken.

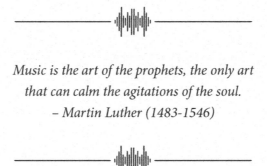

Music is the art of the prophets, the only art
that can calm the agitations of the soul.
– Martin Luther (1483-1546)

Joel 3:10 says it best. "Let the weak say, I am strong." That's not lying. The scripture tells us emphatically that we will possess what we talk about. We have what we say.

We've looked at James 3:2-4 before, but let's take another look in *The Message:*

> Don't be in any rush to become a teacher, my friends. Teaching is highly responsible work. Teachers are held to the strictest standards. And none of us is perfectly qualified. We get it wrong nearly every time we open our mouths. If you could

find someone whose speech was perfectly true, you'd have a perfect person, in perfect control of life.

A bit in the mouth of a horse controls the whole horse. A small rudder on a huge ship in the hands of a skilled captain sets a course in the face of the strongest winds. A word out of your mouth may seem of no account, but it can accomplish nearly anything—or destroy it!

Our destiny is not some mysterious secret in the mind of God, leaving us on the outside guessing and wondering. Our lives are shaped and guided by the creative words of our mouths, bringing life to body, soul, and spirit. Song, saturated with the frequencies of God found in His Word, provides a true compass for the believer and daily help to connect the dots leading to our ultimate best life.

The power of words is amazing. Jesus, the Lord of Glory, is saying, "Life is voice activated. I've given you the gift of choice, to choose the words you speak that will determine every facet of your life."

In other words, you write your own ticket in life.

Jesus said that He only did and said what He *heard* His father do and say. What a great example for us to follow.

Humans were created to be social creatures. The point of the spear in social interaction is being able to converse with others through the course of human events, especially during stressful scenarios.

Isolation is a huge stress producer. Pride, personal guilt, and unforgiveness can be causes of quiet isolation. We were designed to be talkers and listeners. If either of those is out of balance, destructive levels of stress occur.

There are great advantages to facing adversity with others. Yes, we all have individual strengths and skills, but the ideal is to work within an integrated team to achieve the maximum positive result. A well known acronym explains it best:

T. Together

E. Everyone

A. Achieves

M. Much

What is stressful to one person may not be stressful to another. A cross-pollination of strengths, knowledge and experience is a balanced and desirable position to be in.

Words are the key ingredient in making all this work together in a positive way. This is one of the main reasons the enemy of our souls works overtime to keep us offended at one another. Destructive words, or even worse, *no* words can be harmful. In a word vacuum, hearers always mind read in the negative.

You've probably heard the phrase, "The sounds of love don't just happen." Love, like everything else on the planet is word dependent. Visible action expresses love through tasks, but relationship-dependent words penetrate the heart and create an audio adhesive that can be internalized, remembered, and referred to again and again for strength and healing.

History is made up of words and visuals. So, talk. Vent your feelings to trusted listeners. Listen with care to the sounds of life. Every word can be a positive deposit or a painful withdrawal from the bank of life. Our internal search for significance is determined in large part by the words we hear and believe about ourselves.

In the *Amplified Bible* Hebrews 10:25 says, "not forsaking our meeting together [as believers for worship and instruction], as is the habit of some, but encouraging *one another*; and all the more [faithfully] as you see the day [of Christ's return] approaching."

In the original Greek, the implication here is that we are only complete when we get together to fellowship, discuss, pray, eat, share, learn, and make deposits into the lives of others. Words, going out and coming in, connect lives together to make all this happen.

Sound can be defined in many ways. Many definitions and synonymous meanings are dependent upon the context being used. Because we are journeying into a study of the relationship between the natural aspects and the supernatural aspects of sound, we will define sound from a physics perspective.

Sound is mechanical radiant energy expressed in longitudinal pressure waves in a material medium such as air, liquid, or solid. It originates from energy generating sources, is perceived by auditory receptors and transmitted to the brain where it is categorized and analyzed to benefit the hearer as needed.

All Sound is Meaningful

Let's look at a few ways the Bible describes sound.

"There are, it may be, so many kinds of sounds in the world, and none of them is without meaning," (1 Corinthians 14:10 WEB).

Young's Literal Translation says, "There are, it may be, so many kinds of voices in the world, and none of them is unmeaning."

The *King James Version* says, "There are, it may be, so many kinds of voices in the world, and none of them is without signification."

*Harmony sinks deep into the recesses of the
soul and takes its strongest hold there, bringing grace also
to the body and mind as well. Music is moral law. It gives
a soul to the universe, wings to the mind, flight to the
imagination, a charm to sadness, and life to everything.
It is the essence of order.*
– Plato (429-347BC)

All sound is significant.

There is no meaningless sound.

Think about that in relation to your own home. All sound is going to exist for good or evil. What sounds are prevalent in your life?

As we've discussed, God created light first. What followed was illumination, ambient glory, and Shekinah glory. In other words, God's Shekinah glory illuminated everything for the first four days. On the fourth day God made the sun, moon and stars.

Another way to look at it is this: *Only God Himself predates sound.*

That's why your words are so important. They are not idle, nonproductive, meaningless words. There is no such thing.

They are containers of creative power, good or evil.

All of life follows this "sound first" blueprint. Most of the time, you hear something, and then you look. Sound is everywhere, all the time, touching everything. It networks, connects, and weaves all things together. It affects change in everything it touches.

Sound is the audio track that accompanies all the video of life, as infinite as the very voice of God. It interprets what we see and gives it meaning, helping us to respond in the correct way to every stimulus.

Spending quality time feeding on God's Word and developing a lifestyle of worship and prayer will download the divine frequencies necessary to bring life to the body, soul, and spirit through God-saturated words coming out of our mouths. The promises of God contain all that is needed for a life filled with abundant blessings. Meditation on these promises gets them into our hearts. Whatever is in our hearts in abundance will eventually come pouring out of our mouths. Those words will set into motion what is contained within them. We are living today the life that was created by yesterday's words and songs.

CHAPTER TEN

THE HUMAN VOICE

Choice determines the motive, usage and destination of all music. It is the key issue. Music can bring a supernatural peace to our minds. It can relax and heal our bodies, open our human spirits to receive from God. It can help download God's destiny for our lives.

Music, especially music released from our hearts as worship to God, carries within it a deep divine connection. This connection provides for the worshipper not only a great expression of love and gratitude to Him, but God returns that love to us. He pours revelation into His people, as well as His divine peace and joy.

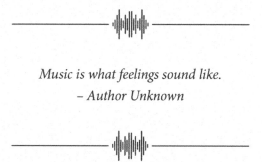

Music is what feelings sound like.
– Author Unknown

God is love. To express Himself, He must have access. We create access to God through our worship, giving Him a pipeline through which to impart His plans, purposes, and pursuits. He gives us wisdom and revelation. His Spirit leads us. This comes directly from God's heart and is always confirmed in God's Word. We move forward, possessing inside information, always coming from a position of strength. This is God's blueprint and His design from the beginning of time, full of blessing, excitement, and freedom.

A Pattern from Heaven

Like the seraphim, the universe and all creation seem to be in constant praise and worship to the Holy One. The pattern in the throne room is repeated in the skies, the earth, and the deepest oceans – everything making music and praising God.

Until man made the wrong choice.

No discussion of sound would be complete without looking at what happened to Lucifer in Heaven. We're told in Ezekiel 28:13 that Lucifer was dazzling to look at and had all the musical instruments of worship built into his being. He was heaven's worship leader.

Angels were given a choice about how they were going to act. Lucifer rebelled, wanting to be worshiped. He aspired to take over the throne of God. For this he was expelled from Heaven.

We read about his fall in Isaiah 14:11-14:

> Your pomp is brought down to Sheol,
>
> *And* the sound of your stringed instruments;
>
> The maggot is spread under you,
>
> And worms cover you.'
>
> "How you are fallen from heaven,
>
> O Lucifer, son of the morning! How you are cut down to the ground,
>
> You who weakened the nations!
>
> For you have said in your heart:
>
> 'I will ascend into heaven,
>
> I will exalt my throne above the stars of God;
>
> I will also sit on the mount of the congregation
>
> On the farthest sides of the north;

I will ascend above the heights of the clouds,

I will be like the Most High.'

Lucifer was stripped of his personal ability to make the sounds of music. It's clear though that his influence over music is palpable, especially as the divine timeline brings him closer to his eternal place of residence. It's very simple. Musical sound has a twofold purpose: To glorify God—or not.

Now that Lucifer, who is also called Satan, has been relieved of his heavenly duties, the job of worship has been turned over to—*us.*

We use external instruments to worship God. The one remaining internal instrument, which is the most powerful of them all, is the *human voice.*

Our voices became the primary instrument of praise and worship.

There are a few interesting facts about sounds produced by the human voice. By definition, the human voice is the "sound made by vibration of vocal folds modified by the resonance of the vocal track."[13] This can be expressed in talking, singing, laughing, crying, or screaming. The three parts of the vocal mechanism are the lungs, the vocal folds (cords) within the larynx, and the articulators, which include the tongue, palate, cheeks and lips. Head size, sinuses, bone structure and other structural influences determine tone and timbre.

[In] sound itself, there is a readiness to be ordered by
the spirit and this is seen at its most sublime in music.
– Max Picard

In martial arts, there is a sharp, powerful battle cry called the *kiai* (pronounced KEY-EYE). It's released with full energy at the split second of contact with an opponent. It is said to harness and focus the attacker's strength in a precise burst of power, breaking up the opponent's focus and releasing a microburst of adrenaline to help prevail over the opponent. The Japanese meaning of *kiai* is "fighting spirit" or "spirit wind."

Accomplished martial arts masters have been known to stun birds and other animals with their *kiais,* much like a dolphin stunning fish with a sonic blast.

In the book, *e-Learning and the Science of Instruction: Pioneer Guidelines for Consumers,* by Ruth C. Clark and Richard E. Mayer, we're told, "research has shown people respond more and learn more quickly and completely when the voice doing the instruction is a human voice and not a robotic voice."

My take? Texting and voice activated texting are great. Just don't forget how to talk. God and His human creation are not cyborgs. We're designed for relationships with God and other humans.

In a report by Megan Holohan, they discovered that babies in the womb can hear and process the sound of their mothers' voices as early as 29 weeks. In a closely monitored experiment, it was shown that babies in utero who listened to CDs of their mothers' voices showed signs of greater brain development, early bonding, and better general cognitive profiles.[14]

Like bonding with the sounds of a mother's voice, God has given each of us a receptor in our human spirit that recognizes His still, small voice within. The Holy Spirit, who is the Spirit of Truth, continues bringing information from the heart of God across our human spirits. The world calls it a hunch or intuition. For the Christian believer it is a constant in our lives.

We need to develop sensitivity to the Voice because it always leads to help, joy, protection, prosperity, life, and strength. Filling our hearts and minds with God's Word will refine our ability to hear this Voice. Worship adds a razor's edge to our inward hearing.

In an article on "Infant Recognition of Mother's Voice," we learned the following: Each of a group of one-month-old infants was reinforced, contingent upon nonnutritive sucking, with its mother's voice and the voice of a stranger. In this experiment, two conditions were applied. Under the first, the mother's speech was aimed at communicating with the infant, while, under the second, the mother's speech lacked prosodic and intonational aspects of normal speech. It was shown that infants will suck more for their mother's voices under the intonated condition only. It was concluded that a young infant prefers its own mother's voice provided the mother speaks normally.[15]

Babies need the musicality of their mother's voice to get the love and bonding necessary for their development. Robotic sounds can't convey these qualities. It's a well known fact in child development circles that unborn children begin to feel and hear the tone, inflections and voiceprint of their mothers' voices. They recognize their fathers' and siblings' voices as well. Musical melodies can be heard and logged into the memory many weeks before birth.

Just like babies in the womb recognize their mother's voice, we too are imprinted by God our Father at the very moment we were formed in the womb.

Deep in the recesses of every human is the ability to know His Voice and the ability to sing His praises in the very key of all creation.

The choice is ours.

While we are on the subject of children in the womb, there is breaking news about the discovery of something extraordinary that happens at the moment of conception. "For the first time ever scientists have captured images of a flash of light that sparks at the very moment a human sperm cell makes contact with an egg. In brief, the egg stores up thousands of compartments of zinc to aid in the viability of the embryo at fertilization. The calcium in the sperm activates the zinc to the point of light-emitting sparks now detectable to advanced video abilities. This" light show" continues for approximately two hours. It has been discovered that the longer the sparks fly the stronger the new embryo becomes. (Bec Crew, 27 April 2016, www.sciencealert.com)

Throughout the cosmos, wherever there is light energy being released, there is always corresponding sound. The genesis pattern is on display once again. The flash of divine light at conception has been proven. Could it be there is an accompanying sound as yet *not* detected? Here we are once again: Sound and light from God are the power twins of creation.

The sperm and the egg are, by design, laden with DNA and are encoded with a complete payload of data with which to build this precious one-of-a-kind human. "Before I formed you in the womb I knew you and before you were born I consecrated you... Jeremiah 1:5 ESV) This includes God's choice of gender and countless other intentional unique qualities that will form this person's entire being.

If God knew us before the womb, where were we? All along we have been in the heart and mind of God. As is His divine pattern, sound and light brought us from the realm of possibilities into the world of physical tangibility, complete with an assigned destiny.

CHAPTER ELEVEN

MIRACLES IN SOUND

One hundred thousand people lifted their voices to God as I led worship in Soweto, South Africa in the early 1980s. The outdoor platform I stood on was over 50 feet tall, and I had a sweeping view of everything before me. I sang a very moving worship song with the words from Isaiah 6, "Holy, Holy, Holy…"

As I sang, something caught my eye. I looked down to my right and saw a man floating up in the air in a seated position. His eyes closed, he seemed unaware that gravity no longer held him in his chair. He was one of the few Caucasians in the audience, so he didn't go unnoticed.

I continued singing because I was aware that somehow, whatever was happening to him was being borne on the wings of the words and music we all sang. After a few seconds, he realized that he was suspended about 10 feet off the ground. He let out a loud shriek.

The moment he did so, he was flung about 25 feet through the air and hit a tall corrugated steel wall that bordered the stage. When he hit the wall, it sounded like a cannon shot. He hit the ground and was instantly surrounded by our security team and several audience members.

As I finished the song, he was ushered up the steps to the platform. The leader of the meeting brought him center stage and handed him a microphone.

"What happened to you?"

The massive crowd fell silent when he tried to speak. At first, his speech was interrupted by a language that he didn't know. Shaken, he told his story.

"I'm a former soldier in the army of Zimbabwe," he explained. "I've been conscripted to fight in a war in Angola. Many of my brothers in arms have been coming back to our duty station different."

After a long pause, he continued. "They said they'd been born again. These are men's men, and I knew it had to be real for all of them to tell us the same story. I came to Johannesburg to visit my girlfriend. I heard about this meeting, and decided to attend to find out for myself about this God and Jesus thing.

"When the crowd was singing 'Holy, Holy, Holy,' I had my eyes closed because I felt something. I didn't want to open my eyes because I was afraid that I would see Jesus. I felt something move, and I opened my eyes. That's when I realized that I was floating in mid-air."

"What happened then?" the leader asked.

"I felt something *big* grab me and throw me up against the wall like I was a stick! Before I even hit the ground, Jesus came into my heart, and I was filled with the Holy Spirit, healed of an old gunshot wound and given direction for the rest of my life."

The whole place went wild. It erupted in praise and dancing.

Worship to God in song provides a sonic conveyance for the power and love of God to manifest.

Very late that night, I was getting ready for bed in my hotel room. I laughed out loud as I remembered what happened to that man. "Lord," I asked, "why did you do that the way you did?"

I didn't hear an audible voice, but inside my spirit, I heard these words as if spoken with a huge grin. "That's the only thing he would understand. Pure power!"

It's very smart to allow God to work out the details in these situations. He sees the big picture and knows the heart of every man.

Sounds of a Miracle

In a similar open air meeting, there were 300,000 in attendance. The sound system was very powerful, the speakers mounted on 100-foot poles, broadcasting in every direction so that everyone could hear. People were being prayed for *en masse* for healing from the platform.

There was a stir near the platform steps as ushers and security guards helped an older man up onto the platform. He was crying as he lifted two old wooden crutches in the air.

"What happened to you?" the leader asked.

"I was waiting for a bus beneath a street lamp," he said mentioning his location five miles away. "The traffic noise around me lowered and all of a sudden I heard a voice booming from out of the sky, 'Be healed in the mighty name of Jesus!'

"Something hit me like a big wave of electricity and knocked me backwards onto the sidewalk. All my pain was instantly gone. I could stand up on my two legs without crutches. I had heard that there was a big meeting here but just physically couldn't get here. I took the next bus here to the meeting. I just had to tell someone!"

He couldn't hear anything from the meeting until the phrase, "Be healed in the mighty name of Jesus!" The wind changed, the sound was carried to his ears more than five miles away, and he joined the thousands who received miracles that night!

*The inoculation effect found in the civilized world
desensitizes us to the voice of God and causes us to miss
the benefits of the supernatural revelation information
His voice carries. As we trade in our close walk with God
for short cuts, substitutes and shallow synthetics, we come
away as dead and empty faith shadows that cannot love,
speak truth, feel, comfort, or heal human hearts.*
– Len Mink

Supernatural Sonic Superiority

It is believed that the prophet Jeremiah wrote the Old Testament books of 1 and 2 Kings, which give accounts of some of the most dramatic sound-related events ever mentioned in Scripture. I've included several excerpts below from the seventh chapter of 2 Kings, because there are so many profound truths chronicled in this single chapter.

The situation in Samaria was grim. Ben-Hadad, the king of Syria and his army had besieged them. There was a great famine, so bad that starving people were eating their own children. In this chapter, we have a vivid account of many miracles, the demonstration of spiritual laws, and the power of words, both positive and negative. We see the amazing manipulation of natural laws to bring about supernatural deliverance. All of this was launched through the God breathed words of the prophet Elisha. As you read this chapter, notice that everything in the story involves sound.

> Then Elisha said, "Hear the word of the LORD. Thus says the
> LORD: 'Tomorrow about this time a seah of fine flour *shall be
> sold* for a shekel, and two seahs of barley for a shekel, at the

gate of Samaria.' So an officer on whose hand the king leaned answered the man of God and said, 'Look, *if* the LORD would make windows in heaven, could this thing be?"

And he said, "In fact, you shall see *it* with your eyes, but you shall not eat of it."

Now there were four leprous men at the entrance of the gate; and they said to one another, "Why are we sitting here until we die? If we say, 'We will enter the city,' the famine *is* in the city, and we shall die there. And if we sit here, we die also. Now therefore, come, let us surrender to the army of the Syrians. If they keep us alive, we shall live; and if they kill us, we shall only die," (2 Kings 7:1-4).

Elisha prophesied to the elders and leaders that within 24 hours there would be a complete turnaround, with a supernatural wave of abundance. There would be more than enough to eat, and it would be cheap. King Jehoram's right hand man exploded in a vocal epithet of unbelief regarding what Elisha had prophesied. Even more, he spoke against Elisha, whom he considered to be in competition with him for favor with the king.

The scene changed to four lepers who were sick, starving, rejected and hopeless. They were outside the gate because of their leprosy. Around dusk, they all had a thought born of desperation. "In the city, we will starve and die," they reasoned. "Out here, we will die. If we go to the Syrians' camp and surrender, they might kill us. What do we have to lose? They might take pity on us and feed us. Why sit here until we die?"

That question was a great declaration of faith which began a sonic miracle.

And they rose at twilight to go to the camp of the Syrians; and when they had come to the outskirts of the Syrian camp, to their surprise no one *was* there. For the Lord had caused the army of the Syrians to *hear* the *noise* of chariots and the *noise* of horses—the *noise* of a great army; so they said to one another, "Look, the king of Israel has hired against us the kings of the Hittites and the kings of the Egyptians to attack us!"

Therefore they arose and fled at twilight, and left the camp intact—their tents, their horses, and their donkeys—and they fled for their lives. And when these lepers came to the outskirts of the camp, they went into one tent and ate and drank, and carried from it silver and gold and clothing, and went and hid *them;* then they came back and entered another tent, and carried *some* from there *also,* and went and hid *it,* (2 Kings 7:5-9, emphasis mine).

Then they said to one another, "We are not doing right. This day *is* a day of good news, and we remain silent. If we wait until morning light, some punishment will come upon us. Now therefore, come, let us go and tell the king's household," (2 Kings 7:5-9).

Just as Elisha had prophesied, the famine was broken and food was cheap. In the rush of the people to get to the spoils, the officer who had spoken against Elisha was trampled to death.

The armies that surrounded them had fled because God caused them to *hear the sound* of chariots and horses. They believed that a great army was on its way. They made their escape, leaving everything behind.

Praise Shouts, "It's Already Done!"

Most of us aren't facing a slow death by starvation like those lepers were. But too often our daily struggles and responsibilities try to suffocate our worship to God. When we gather with others for the praise and worship part of the service, we sometimes just go through the motions, our hearts detached. We don't always feel like worshiping because of rough circumstances.

Verbal and musical praise to God for all He has done and for Who He is, is the shortest pathway to living an overcoming life. Refusing to put your whole heart into praising God is like holding yourself hostage. You become trapped in the troubles that surround you.

*Music is a mixed mathematical science that
concerns the origins, attributes, and distinctions of sound,
out of which a cultivated and lovely melody and harmony
are made, so that God is honored and praised but mankind
is moved to devotion, virtue, joy and sorrow.*
*– Christopher Wolff, Johann Sebastian Bach:
The Learned Musician*

Free, demonstrative, purposeful praise and worship is one of the greatest activities to get your mind off yourself and back onto God. Praise decentralizes and realigns your spiritual self. When that happens, self-pity departs.

I read once that, "Self-pity is spiritual suicide. It is an indefensible self-mutilation of the soul."[16] That is true, and you can't stay in self-pity while you praise and worship your Creator.

The answer to self-pity is made clear in the Bible.

Psalm 35:28 tells us, "And my tongue shall speak of Your righteousness *And* of Your praise all the day long."

> Psalm 150:2 says this, "Praise Him for His mighty acts; Praise
> Him according to His excellent greatness!"

Praise drives out the enemy's influences.

"Now when they began to sing and to praise, the LORD set ambushes against the people of Ammon, Moab, and Mount Seir, who had come against Judah; and they were defeated," (2 Chronicles 20: 22).

Praise crowds out the temptation to complain and get sympathy and attention from others. "Bless the LORD, O my soul, and forget not all His benefits: who forgives all your iniquities, who heals all your diseases, who redeems your life from destruction, who crowns you with lovingkindness and tender mercies," (Psalm 103:2-4).

"Therefore by Him let us continually offer the sacrifice of praise to God, that is, the fruit of *our* lips, giving thanks to His name," (Hebrews 13:15).

Ephesians 1:3 says, "Blessed *be* the God and Father of our Lord Jesus Christ, who has blessed us with every spiritual blessing in the heavenly *places* in Christ."

We're told in Psalm 100:4, "Enter into His gates with thanksgiving, *And* into His courts with praise. Be thankful to Him, *and* bless His name."

God's presence and manifestations of love are drawn to our atmosphere of praise and worship. "But You *are* holy, Enthroned in the praises of Israel," (Psalm 22:3).

One of my personal favorites is found in I Peter 2:9, "But you *are* a chosen generation, a royal priesthood, a holy nation, His own special people, that you may proclaim the praises of Him who called you out of darkness into His marvelous light."

Praise Refreshes

We are refreshed and renewed in His presence.

"Say to God, "How awesome are Your works! Through the greatness of Your power Your enemies shall submit themselves to You. All the earth shall worship You and sing praises to You; they shall sing praises *to* Your name," (Psalm 63:3-4).

"You will show me the path of life; in Your presence *is* fullness of joy; at Your right hand *are* pleasures forevermore," (Psalm 16:11).

The Bible tells us what happens when we praise God with our whole hearts:

"I will praise *You,* O LORD, with my whole heart;

I will tell of all Your marvelous works.

I will be glad and rejoice in You;

I will sing praise to Your name, O Most High.

When my enemies turn back,

They shall fall and perish at Your presence.

For You have maintained my right and my cause;

You sat on the throne judging in righteousness. (Psalm 9:1-4)"

"I will call upon the LORD, *who is worthy* to be praised; so shall I be saved from my enemies," (Psalm 18:3).

Thanksgiving also strengthens our faith. The Lord said this about Abraham, "He did not waver at the promise of God through unbelief, but was strengthened in faith, giving glory to God, (Romans 4:20).

Praise helps us cast off oppression. "Why are you cast down, O my soul? And why are you disquieted within me? Hope in God; For I shall yet praise Him, The help of my countenance and my God," (Psalm 42:11).

Everything in the Kingdom of God is associated with faith. Yet, often we face tough situations in financial arenas, physical challenges, acute fatigue, or problems within our families. When we praise Him in the face of over-whelming odds, we are declaring and decreeing by faith our own dominance over these would-be assassins of our lives.

Faith is the core, the central issue of worship that lifts the believer from the strict dictates and confines of battle into the already accomplished position of victory that we enjoy in Jesus.

Praise brings the benefits of those victories won by Christ into the present. When you praise God for what He has already done, it changes everything.

> *It's already done;*
>
> *It's already done.*
>
> *Jesus has done it;*
>
> *The battle is won!*

CHAPTER TWELVE

THE ANGEL ON ASSIGNMENT

I ascended the steps to the platform to lead worship at Kenneth Copeland Ministries Believers' Convention on August 10, 1995. I'd known all day that this night would be out of the ordinary. I'd felt a growing sense of excitement, and I'd also experienced a strange sense of heaviness in my legs. I prayed, as I always did, about what songs to use as worship that evening. Toward the end of the list were two songs that I felt the Lord wanted sung into the atmosphere. One was the hymn "Holy, Holy, Holy," and the other was a masterpiece by Bill and Gloria Gaither, "There's Something About That Name."

Thousands of believers filled the convention center in Fort Worth, Texas, and raised their voices in praise and worship to God. When we started singing "Holy, Holy, Holy," the presence of the Lord swept through the auditorium like a tsunami. The words of the second verse said, "Cherubim and Seraphim falling down before thee…"

As I sang those words, something caught my eye at stage left above the television lights. It glowed with more light than the lighting system. I got out a few words, and then I couldn't continue. The glory of God was so great that I had to hold onto the pulpit to keep from falling. I blinked over and over trying to get a better look.

A being 10 or 12 feet tall hung suspended about 30 feet off the floor just in front of the balcony. It had a human silhouette that radiated pure, perfect light. It was free of any earthly filters or light-wave altering particles.

As the being came into focus, I could tell it wasn't generating the light. Rather, it reflected the light from some other source. I didn't know light could be that free of imperfections. Other than the undulating light, the creature's body was motionless except that its head moved, scanning from side to side, as though recording our event.

On top of its head, tendrils of colorless fire without impurities floated upward and outward. I thought there was a headband around its forehead. Then, when I looked again, I saw that it was many individual eyes encircling the top of its head. The eyes were dark and shiny, about the size of golf balls. His face was bronze and gray-colored with flat chiseled facets, and two larger deep eyes that looked like black fire.

Its mouth was small and pursed, as though its jaw was clinched. The light on its face changed constantly like a 3D image, revealing other features that I'm unable to categorize in earth terms. The best way to describe those features is beast-like.

The amazing strength of the creature was vivid. He had no neck, except to say that it was nothing but muscle, sinew and undulating ligaments, much like a body builder. I expected to see shoulders with arms. Instead, there were shimmering, wavy, multi-colored wing-looking things coming out from each shoulder. Each was about 20 feet in length.

They looked like the aurora borealis, the northern lights seen in winter skies in the north. Massive arms and hands came out from where the ribcage would be in a human body. The arms and hands appeared to be so strong that the creature could take an entire planet in its hands and turn it into cosmic dust with a squeeze.

Falling Under the Glory

At that point, I felt totally overloaded on every level. Both the Old and New Testaments tell of people who fell to the ground in the strong presence of God. Here are some examples.

Abram fell when God spoke to him (Gen 17:3).

- Joshua fell when he experienced the presence of the Lord (Joshua 5:14-15).

- Ezekiel fell when the glory of the Lord appeared to him (Ezekiel 1:28; 3:23).

- Daniel fell on the ground when he encountered the glory of God (Daniel 8:17; 10:15).

- When God's glory was manifested to Peter, James and John, all three fell to the ground (Matt 17:6).

- Paul fell on the earth when he saw Christ on the road to Damascus (Acts 9:4; 26:14).

- John fell at the feet of Jesus at the beginning of his vision on the isle of Patmos. It says that John fell as one dead. The word dead in Greek is *nekros* which is the word for corpse. It seems that all the life had gone from John, making him fall forward, which is *piptos* in Greek, at the feet of Jesus.[17]

- I identified with the biblical accounts of people not being able to stand in the heavy atmosphere of God's presence. The Hebrew word *kavod* (k-v-d) means weight, heaviness, honor, respect or majesty. In the Strong's Hebrew Lexicon, the primary meaning is glory or weighty glory.

I believe that at times like these all human senses operate at an elevated level. I noticed many things in those 10 or 12 minutes that would normally be filtered by distractions and human reasoning.

There is an ultimate note in the heart of the Christian. It is the note of conscious victory through Jesus Christ. The nearer our life is tuned to that note of conscious victory, the greater the victory that will be evidenced in our life.
– John G. Lake

I glanced at the audience several times and noticed something I'd never seen before in a worship gathering. I heard 10,000 singing people being overwhelmed by the power of God. A holy hush fell. It was thick and palpable with occasional scattered sounds of people crying. Then I heard a wave of the sound of chairs moving. It sounded like sacks of potatoes dropping to the floor.

I'd seen thousands of people in prayer lines fall backwards when hands were laid on them. This time, though, as my gaze swept over the crowd, I saw hundreds of people falling, and without exception, they all fell *forward*, prostrate before God.

I looked up at the creature still hovering above the TV lights and noticed that it was brighter than before. He seemed to be wearing a long, hanging garment made of folded, pleated light.

I distinctly heard the Holy Spirit say, "Now, sing 'Jesus, There's Something About That Name.'" I turned and nodded to our pianist, David Ellis. While waiting for his first notes to begin the song, I sang the first "Jesus." Then I sang the second "Jesus," and my eyes went back to the creature. As I sang the name of Jesus, our visitor from Heaven bowed his huge head, brought in his outstretched wings, and wrapped them around his entire being. He buried his face in his chest, looking something like a giant glistening cocoon.

That was it for me.

I was undone. I thought that I was going to leave the earth at that moment.

The Assignment

I glanced over and saw Jesse Duplantis worshiping on the front row with his head bowed. I brought the microphone to my lips and whispered, "Jesse, please come here and help me."

Jesse made his way to the center platform, and I handed him the microphone.

"Ladies and gentlemen," he said, "there is obviously an angel sent from God to this meeting for a purpose, an assignment."

Looking up toward the area where my gaze had been fixed, he said with reverent authority. "Messenger of God, we release you to complete your assignment from God, in Jesus' name!"

Suddenly, the creature compressed into a razor thin light of intense cobalt blue. Then it exploded, passing everywhere and through everyone in the convention center. Afterwards, he passed through the walls and was gone.

Someone helped me off the stage as Kenneth Copeland made his way to center stage to continue the flow of the supernatural atmosphere.

Since that night in 1995, we've had a continuing stream of people recounting what happened to them. This book couldn't hold all the stories we've heard. I've never seen miracles happen on so many levels. There have been numerous reports of audience members being healed during those few short minutes when time seemed to stand still.

A young man from Russia was volunteering as an usher that night, working in the balcony nearest the angelic being. Near the end of the visitation, he moved away from his area to find a place to sit. He felt like he was going to fall. As he moved back, he described hitting a force field. Something grabbed him, pulling him into that force.

*Nothing will align the human entity with the Divine
more quickly and accurately than praise and worship in
song. The plans, purposes, and pursuits of God are tapped
into and coordinated with the spiritual and natural GPS
transmitted from God directly into each believer.*
– Len Mink

In an instant, he was healed and delivered. He told me that in Russia as a young child, he'd been molested by a priest at his parish. A spirit of homosexuality was transferred to him.

He'd struggled with that spirit for years, and at one time he contemplated suicide.

In the split second in the force field, he told me he was delivered completely from homosexuality. His back was healed from a serious injury, and he received details about what to do for the rest of his life.

A pastor and his wife were considering divorce. They each came to the meeting, neither knowing that the other was there. During that intense event, they somehow saw one another in the crowd of over 10,000 people. They locked eyes and then ran to one another. They were reconciled in that moment.

Everything that happened that night was miraculous, dripping with God's love and power. What happened defies explanation. For instance, several people came to the meeting the following morning wearing the same clothes they wore the night before. None of them had any idea where they'd been all night.

When we returned home to Tulsa, we had a private meeting with Kenneth E. Hagin. He listened to our story and leaned back in his chair with his hands folded in his lap. With a twinkle in his eyes he said, "It sounds like one of the four living creatures around God's throne mentioned in Revelation 4:6-8."

> Before the throne *there was* a sea of glass, like crystal. And in the midst of the throne, and around the throne, *were* four living creatures full of eyes in front and in back. The first living creature *was* like a lion, the second living creature like a calf, the third living creature had a face like a man, and the fourth living creature *was* like a flying eagle. *The* four living creatures, each having six wings, were full of eyes around and within. And they do not rest day or night, saying: "Holy, holy, holy, Lord God Almighty, Who was and is and is to come!"

Soon afterwards, we spoke to Charles Capps, and he agreed with Kenneth Hagin.

Well known prophet, psalmist, and teacher, Vicki Jameson, sat on the front row during the visitation. She said, "Len, as you sang, I saw brightly colored musical notes, lots of them, coming out of your mouth, streaming upward toward heaven."

In retrospect, I believe that the choice of those two songs, "Holy, Holy, Holy" and "There's Something About That Name" with their specific divine frequencies created an atmosphere for the visitation.

Should you look for angels? I would advise against it. Too often, believers want a sign, an over the top confirmation from God, instead of believing His Word and walking by faith.

Are you an angel hunter? Do you need special signs before you can believe? If so, the enemy will accommodate you. What you encounter may wow you at first, then lead you down a path you do *not* want to follow.

Supernatural visitations are great if it's God's idea, with His timing and confirming the Word of God. Signs and wonders are always exciting, but only the Word of God can give and develop your faith and character. Otherwise, you're like someone driving at night with your lights turned off.

Principles of Worship

It's been my great privilege to have been the worship leader for Kenneth Copeland Ministries for more than four decades. It's been a rich, ever-revealing journey of discovery and amazing manifestations of the glory of God. Over the years, there have been four major worship priorities that have guided me in achieving the exchange between God and man, resulting in the glory of God changing countless lives.

First Worship Principle: Give God the glory due His name.

This principle is based in part on Psalm 29:2 from the *Jewish Publication Society Bible.*

"Ascribe unto the Lord the glory due His name; worship the Lord in the beauty of holiness." [18]

Second Worship Principle: Give God's people a rich worship experience.

One of the primary reasons people want to come to a worship event is to sense the mighty presence of God. They want to leave stronger and more on course than when they came. They want to find answers and to receive courage and strength to live an overcoming life. A. W. Tozer said, "True and absolute freedom is only found in the presence of God."

In Psalm 16:11 we are told, "You will show me the path of life; in Your presence *is* fullness of joy; at Your right hand *are* pleasures forevermore."

Third Worship Principle: Prepare the pulpit for the one delivering the Word of Life.

You prepare the atmosphere and then hand the gathering over to them at the highest possible point of inspiration and expectancy. When they take the stage, the spiritual momentum created by worship will catapult them into a free and unhindered atmosphere of the glory of God.

In one form or another, the one speaking is to continue the earthly ministry of Jesus as found in Isaiah 61:1-3:

"The Spirit of the Lord GOD *is* upon Me, because the LORD has anointed Me
To preach good tidings to the poor;
He has sent Me to heal the brokenhearted,
To proclaim liberty to the captives,
And the opening of the prison to *those who are* bound;
To proclaim the acceptable year of the LORD,
And the day of vengeance of our God;
To comfort all who mourn,
To console those who mourn in Zion,
To give them beauty for ashes,
The oil of joy for mourning,
The garment of praise for the spirit of heaviness;
That they may be called trees of righteousness,
The planting of the LORD, that He may be glorified."

At the appropriate place and at the speaker's direction, worship may be continued to affirm and ratify the Word of God. It will seal the work of the Holy Spirit in the heart of each believer. The worship offered before the Word is preached must put wind beneath the wings of the speaker.

Fourth Worship Principle: Know when to disappear.

This is perhaps the most important aspect of leading others in worship before God. Knowing the exact moment to hand the service over to the one ministering the Word of God, the gifts of the Spirit, or the direction the Holy Spirit is leading.

It's time for the worship leader to disappear. Get out of sight. You must remove your influence to make room for the next thing God wants to do. Successful ministry is always a relay event. Don't grip your baton with your need for attention, your indecisiveness, or your lack of confidence. During the angelic visitation, I knew when the Lord wanted me to turn the service over to Jesse Duplantis. When that happens, you blend into the shadows and release the Holy Spirit to move as He wishes through the leader now responsible for the service.

Luke 14:11 explains it best, "For whoever exalts himself will be humbled, and he who humbles himself will be exalted."

I believe that there are certain times when God wants to meet with His people and impart to us. The Bible mentions many appointed moments in time, which God uses to accomplish important things. In Hebrew, they're called *moedim*, which means appointed times.

August 10, 1995 was an appointed time.

God doesn't seem so concerned about *time* as He does about His *timing*.

The consensus among the leaders who were there and those with whom I have since shared the experience is that the angelic creature was sent to gather, record, document, and take a report to Heaven. It had everything to do with God's grand plan, from the big prophetic picture all the way to each of us walking in God's perfect will for our lives.

CHAPTER THIRTEEN

THE CROSSFIRE

In my continuing desire to plumb the depths of worship, I've discovered a seldom discussed, recurring principle—a spiritual law. There is something I call the crossfire. It seems to govern the world of sound, especially when words and music are combined. When that happens, they gain strength exponentially, the music acting as a lubricant to carry the DNA of the word frequencies deep into the human heart.

There, they begin transmitting their contents throughout the whole person. If this download is uplifting, truthful, and affirming, the effect is positive. If the deposited frequencies are toxic, untruthful, and dark, the outward manifestations will be negative.

What we hear, especially in words accompanied by music, has a direct influence on our success. Because we believe what we hear ourselves say more than we believe what we hear others say, it's incumbent upon us to monitor this powerful exchange of sound-borne data.

This thread of revelation is found in full display in the ever-revealing Word of God. I first caught sight of it in Isaiah chapter six, where Isaiah peered through the curtain of time and eternity and saw an overwhelming sight. Let's take another look at Isaiah 6:1-4:

> In the year that King Uzziah died, I saw the Lord sitting on a throne, high and lifted up, and the train of His *robe* filled the temple. Above it stood seraphim; each one had six wings: with two he covered his face, with two he covered his feet, and with two he flew. And one cried to another and said:
>
> "Holy, holy, holy *is* the LORD of hosts;

The whole earth *is* full of His glory!"

And the posts of the door were shaken by the voice of him
who cried out, and the house was filled with smoke.

Isaiah gave us a detailed account of what he saw. He was very precise in
that he gave us a verifiable time stamp. This happened in the year that King
Uzziah died. Uzziah became king of Judah, which was ancient Israel, at the
age of 16. He reigned for 52 years and died in 740 BC.

According to 2 Chronicles 26:16, Uzziah's power and fame led him to
become proud. He felt that he was above the law of God, so he burned
incense on the altar. That task was reserved for the priesthood, the sons
of Aaron.

Eighty courageous priests confronted him at the altar. As they argued, leprosy broke out on Uzziah's forehead. He ran from the temple in fear and
lived the rest of his life in a separate palace.

I'm including Uzziah's story to underscore the importance of keeping
our hearts and motives pure before God. Doing this shuts the door to the
enemy. We must never steal any of God's glory by being preoccupied with
ourselves during worship and service to God.

Worship leaders, you especially must heed this advice.

Sowing and reaping works in the positive or the negative every time.

Motive determines words spoken. Words determine destinies.

Isaiah's account of Heaven's pattern for praise and worship is almost an
overload for our physical senses. Try to put yourself in Isaiah's sandals as
we discover one of the most powerful revelations in the Word of God.

I'd read this passage many times over the years, but this time the curtain
was pulled back, and I saw something that has changed everything in my
life. In Isaiah 6:1-4, the first verse describes God seated upon the throne,
high and lifted up. His train, also called glory skirts in the *Hebrew Old*

Testament, filled the temple. This was a structured habitation in Heaven, not made with human hands.

Jesus did not heal the sick in order to coax them to be
Christians. He healed because it was His nature to heal.
– John G. Lake

Verse two tells us that above the throne are positioned an ever-moving circular multitude of seraphim, God's attendant angels. The implication is that there are many, many of these beings. The word *seraph* means to burn with zeal, dazzling brightness of appearance, rapidly moving and a hundred percent aware.[19]

Each *seraph* had six wings. Two covered his face, as he was unworthy to look upon God's Person. Two covered his feet and lower parts. Two were in motion, ready for instant flight in God's service. They are in active standby mode. The mention of hands and feet implies a somewhat human form.

One cried to another, "Holy, holy, holy *is* the LORD of hosts; the whole earth *is* full of His glory!" (Isaiah 6:3).

The vibrant, rapidly moving activity that Isaiah describes in this verse pertains to countless heavenly angelic hosts, or warriors. They circle the throne, crying with intense passion, "Holy, Holy, Holy is the LORD [Jehovah] of hosts [heavenly hosts]: the whole earth is full of His glory."

This phrase could be read, "And the whole earth *must be made* to be filled with His glory." These beings are in a shoutfest, face to face with one another, about every facet of God's person. It is very interesting that these heavenly beings are declaring God's glory in the earth, when they are all in Heaven.

"And the posts of the door were shaken by the voice of him who cried out, and the house was filled with smoke," (Isaiah 6:4).

It sounds as though the worship was so loud and intense that Heaven suffered structural damage. Notice that once again the structure is referenced, in this case the posts and the door. This says the posts of the door actually moved!

The smoke was the heavenly atmospheric substance we call glory. The Hebrew word for glory is *kavod*. It is the heavy, intensely alive presence of God.

A Man of Unclean Lips

Notice how Isaiah reacts:

> So I said:
>
> "Woe *is* me, for I am undone!
>
> Because I *am* a man of unclean lips,
>
> And I dwell in the midst of a people of unclean lips;
>
> For my eyes have seen the King,
>
> The LORD of hosts."
>
> Then one of the seraphim flew to me, having in his hand a live coal *which* he had taken with the tongs from the altar. And he touched my mouth *with it,* and said:
>
> "Behold, this has touched your lips;
>
> Your iniquity is taken away,
>
> And your sin purged."

In addition to praising God, the *seraphs* were involved in imparting spiritual fire from God to His prophet. When Isaiah lamented about his own and the peoples' unclean lips, it pertained to speech, words, music and everything that has to do with human audio. In contrast to the pure lips of the seraphim chanting in alternate response, Isaiah suffered a deep sense of his own unfitness to speak God's message to the people.

As he lamented over his unclean condition, we see a beautiful pre-incarnate picture of God's amazing grace through Jesus' sacrifice brought from the future backward into Isaiah's present moment. God sent a *seraph* to the altar of burnt offering in the temple court to retrieve a live coal from the altar. The *seraph* put the coal on Isaiah's mouth and said, "Behold, this has touched your lips; your iniquity is taken away, and your sin purged." What a picture of grace!

The Angels Worship in the Crossfire

If we follow the pattern in Isaiah chapter six, we recognize that God created these angelic beings to engage in a *crossfire of worship*. From each side of the throne, they circle, facing one another. They rave and boast about how holy, awesome, powerful, worthy, and perfect God is. As their praise crosses the throne, it creates an atmosphere of the heavenly substance we call glory between their faces. It was in *that* supercharged atmosphere that God lifted His voice and decreed, "Let there be light!" This is a good place to take another look at the divine process of creation.

"The earth was formless, an empty wasteland, and darkness was upon the face of the deep [primeval ocean that covered the unformed earth]. The Spirit of God was moving (hovering, brooding) over the face of the waters," (Gen 1:2, AMP).

That phrase, "hovering, brooding over the face of the waters," lends itself to an image of the dark, chaotic, primordial waters of the earth being closely watched over by God the Holy Spirit. He is the kinetic agent of change concerning God's will everywhere. An overview of this verse leads me to believe that the phrase "brooding over the deep" could be accurately substituted by saying, "The Holy Spirit was hovering above the disorganized earthly mess, waiting for words filled with divine substance."

When God the Father spoke the words of creation, God the Holy Spirit went to work making tangible manifestations out of the words spoken from God's heart and mouth. The DNA of God, the substance to become manifested, was in each word and song.

By the way, according to the chronological order of creation found in Genesis 1, we know that the sun and stars weren't created until the fourth day. I believe that this very first presence of light was the atmosphere of Glory created in Heaven between the angels' faces. It was the atmosphere that created the ambiance to speak words of life to create earth and the universe. Amazed at the way this crossfire seemed to work, I'd been spending more time in worship, knowing that the angels were with me, creating that crossfire.

I began to practice this in my daily life. One afternoon, Cathy sent me on an errand. On the way to the grocery store, I got the crossfire going with the angels. Inside, I stopped on aisle four and used my quiet voice to continue praising God. The store wasn't too busy, and I lost myself in worship for about 30 minutes. As I praised God, I imagined the angels looking at me as we created a force field.

I heard a noise and looked to the other end of the aisle. A man dropped a small plastic shopping basket and ran toward me. When he reached me, he launched himself into my arms, sobbing. I held him as we both dropped to our knees. I rocked back and forth, as though holding a child, and comforted him. "It's okay," I said. "Whatever it is, it's okay."

After a while, he stopped crying, stood up and dried his face.

"I'm sorry," he said. "So sorry."

"What's going on?"

He took a deep, shuddering breath.

"I've been a pastor," he explained. "I had a moral failure. I lost my wife. My children hate me. Of course, I lost my church. I've survived by installing windows, but that's not what I was created to do. I've been so miserable for so long that I asked God for a sign. I told Him that I was going to buy a frozen turkey dinner and microwave it. Then, if I didn't hear from him, I was going to kill myself.

"When I turned the corner into this aisle, I saw you. Your face was glowing so bright that I couldn't look into it. Your face looked like the way the Bible described Moses' face after he'd met with God and been given the Ten Commandments. It radiated the glory. I knew this was my sign."

I prayed with him on aisle four. Afterwards, I plugged him in with a pastor friend of mine who ministered to the man and got him back on track. Within a year, he was ministering again.

Musicians talk of an ultimate note. That is a note you will not find on any keyboard. It is a peculiar note. A man sits down to tune a piano, or any fine instrument. He has no guide to the proper key, and yet he has a guide. That guide is the note that he has in his soul. The nearer he can bring his instrument into harmony with that note in his soul, the nearer perfection he has attained.
– John G. Lake

It's common knowledge in the world of cosmology that the universe is expanding at an increasing rate of speed. In other words, God's original words have never stopped creating worlds. And the process is accelerating.[20]

There is an extremely important takeaway for us that is a life changer. When we get together as Jesus' followers—as born again, spirt-filled, hungry-for-more believers—a powerful and supernatural thing takes place. Just as the angels in Isaiah chapter six worshiped face to face, shouting praises to God, we gather face to face to proclaim how awesome and precious He is to us.

Between our faces, our worship creates the crossfire, consisting of the heavenly atmospheric substance called glory. It is in this atmosphere that God can manifest all the facets of His character and person.

This is where miracles happen, people are healed, destinies are realized and exponential growth takes place. It's where God pulls you closer into an intimacy with Him that you've only dreamed about.

God does dwell and manifest Himself in His children's worship and praise.

What To Do

In today's lightning paced world of shallow electronic relationships and busy agendas regarding me, myself, and I, it is very difficult to set aside the time to create a clear channel between ourselves and God.

Book some God time on your calendar every day.

Turn off your cell phone and tune in to Him.

Read the Word out loud.

Sing praises, dance for Him, pour out your heart, even if you're upset at your current situation.

Then do the most important thing. Stop and really listen for God's reply.

It will always be straight, true, and filled with grace and life. It will lead you to a higher level of strength and joy.

When you think about this, remember that Lucifer, the most beautiful created angelic being in Heaven, deceived himself into wanting to be like God. He wanted to be worshiped, and he wanted to be in charge.

Ezekiel 28:17a says this about Lucifer, "You thought you were so handsome that it made your heart proud. You thought you were so glorious that it spoiled your wisdom," (NIRV).

So many things can be learned here. I want to point out a seldom discussed dynamic that will empower you to fine tune your spiritual and social smarts.

Lucifer said in his heart five times the words that revealed his rebellious scheme:

I WILL ascend to Heaven.

I WILL raise my throne above the stars of God.

I WILL sit enthroned on the mount of assembly, on the utmost heights of the sacred mountain.

I WILL ascend above the tops of the clouds.

I WILL make myself like the Most High.

These declarations are the framework for the modern-day mantras of secular humanism.

Knowing how this crossfire works, Satan's ploy is to lure us into face to face conversations that are the opposite of what God intends. Satan lures us into word exchanges that involve trash talking about other people, speaking sickness, poverty and death, implying that God can't deliver on the promises in His Word.

Just as God stands in the center of that atmosphere of glory and speaks the words to create and bring life, Satan steps into the trash-talking, hatred generating, fear dependent atmosphere of anti-glory to steal, kill and destroy.

Sometimes I almost slap myself around a little to reinforce the reality that words that I speak eventually come true. Word seeds that I plant will sprout over time. They will grow and bear fruit. The key to this self-fine-tuning exercise is to treat every word as though it will manifest today.

May the crossfires that we take part in always give glory to God. May they create atmospheres that bring forth miraculous things in our lives.

CHAPTER FOURTEEN

RAISING JESUS FROM THE DEAD

I was meditating on the crossfire revelation late one night, when I heard God's voice inside my spirit. He whispered, *"Do you want to know how I raised my Son's physical body from the dead?"*

I almost shot through the ceiling of my study. After pausing for several seconds I said,

"Yes, Sir, I really do."

"It's in John chapter 20."

Excited, I grabbed my Bible and turned there.

The sepulcher where they buried Jesus' body had been sealed. They'd also posted guards around the clock. When Mary arrived, she saw that the stone that covered the grave, which was probably 1,000 pounds or more, had been rolled away. Believing that someone had stolen Jesus' body, she raced to Simon Peter's house, bringing the disciples back with her to the tomb.

Peter arrived last to the sepulcher. Stepping into the vault, he saw the linens lying there, but there was no body. Peter and the other disciples went back to their homes.

When Mary Heard Him

But Mary stayed, standing at the opening of the sepulcher weeping. As she wept, she decided to look inside the burial chamber again. This time, she saw two angels in white. They were sitting, one at the head and one at the feet of where Jesus had been laid.

"Why are you weeping?" one of the angels asked.

"Because they've taken away my Lord, and I don't know where they laid him."

Jesus appeared at the entrance of the tomb. "Woman, why are you crying?"

Thinking he might be the gardener, she asked if he had moved Jesus' body.

When I read the next line, the hair stood up on the back of my neck.

"Mary," He said.

It wasn't until she heard His voice speaking her name that she recognized him.

And that's when it exploded in my spirit.

Crossfire!

God positioned two angels in the sepulcher, one at the head of Jesus' body and one at His feet. They must have praised and worshiped God while looking at one another. Jesus' dead body was between them, caught in the crossfire of their praise. That atmosphere of glory raised Him from the dead. I assume the angels rolled the stone away, because it was wide open when Mary and the disciples arrived.

This revelation is loaded with quantum gems and deep significance.

Do you have a problem?

Do you have a roadblock?

Do you have an impossible situation?

Put it in the crossfire.

Get with your spouse, children, friends or fellow believers and set up a crossfire of worship. Place sickness, poverty, sorrow, lack and barrenness right into the physical middle of a circle of worshiping believers. Watch the miracles flow.

Many people with whom I've shared this truth have put it into action and seen astounding things happen. God does inhabit, dwell in, and manifest Himself in the praises of His people.

Resurrection life is in His presence.

The Rapture

The next thing I want to discuss is a miraculous event that has yet to take place—the great catching away of the Church discussed in 1 Thessalonians 4:16-17:

> For the Lord Himself will descend from heaven with a shout, with the voice of an archangel, and with the trumpet of God. And the dead in Christ will rise first. Then we who are alive *and* remain shall be caught up together with them in the clouds to meet the Lord in the air. And thus we shall always be with the Lord.

Jesus, the King of the Resurrection, will *shout* to all the dead in Christ with the divine frequencies of Creation itself. Every subatomic particle that made up each person will come from wherever it is, gather at His command and reassemble. This is basically a reenactment of Genesis 1:7, God using sound to create and recreate. I contend that this is going to be the employment of every musical frequency used in Genesis.

The Law of Conservation of Matter states that matter, with no regard to particle size or location, can never be destroyed, only changed and rearranged. Like atoms, energy cannot disappear, only relocate.

It's evident that this will be a loud and powerful event both for the dead in Christ and for those who are still alive on earth. In this passage, we see the Lord descending from Heaven with a shout. The word shout used here is one of the most understated translations in Scripture. Calling this sound a shout is similar to standing in front of a locomotive and calling its air horn a little toot.

The Greek word for shout is *keleusmati,* which means a loud command. Notice that this loud command is accompanied by the voice of an archangel. The archangels are royalty in Heaven. They are mighty captains over all the other classes of angels. It appears that the archangel's voice was not embedded within Jesus' vocal command. Rather, it was projected toward the earth, along with the Lord's shout. Keep in mind that this indescribably powerful projection of cosmic sound is the same one that created all matter in the first place.

When talking about raising people from the dead, the question always comes up about people burned, vaporized, decomposed or cremated. How would God recreate them? As previously mentioned, the Law of Conservation of Matter states that matter and energy never go away. They just change form.

I feel quite sure that the God who assembled the cosmos and everything in it can reassemble all the scattered subatomic particles to their original mint condition.

Pause and think about that.

Faith has a song. It rejoices before it sees.
– Len Mink

According to verse 16, the dead in Christ will rise first. It seems as if it all happens in an instant. However, what if it took a while before the living joined the resurrected ones? What a scene that would be. Let your imagination run with that thought for a while. I believe that millions would come to Christ in a few minutes, if there was a last, momentary period of grace.

Verse 17, the Lord returns with a shout, with the voice of an archangel and with the trump of God. There are multiple scripture references to God's voice sounding like the loudest, biggest, and most powerful trumpet ever.

For instance, look at this passage in Exodus 19:16-19. This is the scene just before the Ten Commandments were given to Moses. God's voice sounded like a trumpet, and it was loud.

> Then it came to pass on the third day, in the morning, that there were thunderings and lightnings, and a thick cloud on the mountain; and the sound of the trumpet was very loud, so that all the people who *were* in the camp trembled. And Moses brought the people out of the camp to meet with God, and they stood at the foot of the mountain. Now Mount Sinai *was* completely in smoke, because the LORD descended upon it in fire. Its smoke ascended like the smoke of a furnace, and the whole mountain quaked greatly. And when the blast of the trumpet sounded long and became louder and louder, Moses spoke, and God answered him by voice (Exodus 19:16-19).

The Mountain Shook

God's voice was so forceful that it shook Mount Sinai. Fire and smoke covered the mountain. According to Strong's Concordance #6227, the word *ashan* used here means angry-looking, roiling plumes. Verse 19 says that the sounds of the trumpet got louder and louder. Imagine being from a primitive culture and seeing, hearing and feeling such a violent, loud event. It would have been terrifying.

Without a doubt, Yahweh had their full attention.

John referred to this very same sound in his vision on the Isle of Patmos.

"I was in the Spirit on the Lord's Day, and I heard behind me a loud voice, as of a trumpet," (Rev 1:10).

The first chapter of Revelation tells us that John heard the voice of the resurrected Jesus Christ, seated at the Father's right hand after His ascension. He describes more in the fourth chapter.

"After these things I looked, and behold, a door *standing* open in heaven. And the first voice which I heard *was* like a *trumpet speaking with me*, saying, "Come up here, and I will show you things which must take place after this," (Revelation 4:1 emphasis mine).

Both times that John referred to this experience, he described it as a loud trumpet blast. There was the voice and there was the shaking. The Greek words *salpiggi* or *salpiggo* are used to convey the sound of a trumpet. Those same words were used in 1 Corinthians and 1 Thessalonians to describe the sound just before the dead in Christ are resurrected.

A form of these same Greek words was used when Jesus died and the veil of the temple was torn in two.

"Just then the temple curtain was torn in two, from top to bottom. The earth shook and the rocks were split apart," (Matthew 27:51, NET). The word shook is the Greek word *eseisthe*.

It is the Greek word for our English word, seismic.

Lazarus, Come Out!

The Lord's trumpet blast, shout, or command may have been like the divine frequencies contained in Jesus' words in John 11:43, "Lazarus, come out!"

Lazarus had already been dead four days. His body was decomposing. It would have been stinking, as Martha pointed out to Jesus. The frequencies contained in Jesus' command carried ultimate life into Lazarus' decomposing body, and he came forth from the tomb.

This voice as a trumpet made the dead alive. The Lord can do this for you today in your own life. You may be dealing with barren, stressful, or unhappy areas. If so, take a moment right now and listen for His voice of resurrection and newness of life. Even if you feel swallowed in grave clothes, get up and run toward His loving voice.

We are each like a one-of-a-kind tuning fork.
When we make contact with the world, or the world
touches us, each of us resonates with the frequencies of our
deepest internal self. Tuning forks are used to provide a
tonal baseline for others to tune their instruments.
– Len Mink

Understanding the Trinity Through Music

Many people have attempted the daunting task of trying to understand our triune God.

The ideal way to understand the trinity is through music. Music's core component is the melody. When you add harmony to the melody, the full expanse of the musicscape begins to emerge. With the addition of a third note, we hear all three separately. They form one sound which we call a chord. The notes compliment and amplify one another, creating a sound much fuller and more expressive and powerful than each note alone.

Listen for the fullness of the Voice of God.

CHAPTER FIFTEEN

WHY WE SING

In the delivery room, one of the first things a newborn does is make a sound. He takes his first huge gasp of air—and then he cries. Sound is his first realization. *I have a voice! I can make a sound to get my needs met!*

Each one of us was born with a basic understanding of sound. Even infants arrive hard wired with an affinity for musical notes and tones. The sounds of Brahms's Lullaby or the notes of "Twinkle, Twinkle Little Star" playing from a mobile hanging over a crib make it clear that we have no defense against anything delivered to us through music. Mothers bond and comfort their children by singing, humming, and cooing. Music is used to teach life lessons, information, and identity to almost every child on earth.

In the divine overview, there is perfect harmony, symmetry, and order in the universe. God's Word, which is Divine Providence, sets all the balances and boundaries to that order. It is both the background music and the stage upon which our lives are played out. We create our own unique song by harmonizing with divine melody and filling in specific notes through our free will. Therefore, Divine Providence and our free will harmonize to form both a steady beat and a solo improvisation.

In this way, God sings *through us* to the world.

Each person, though a part of the unified body of Christ, is a world unto himself. We are each a one-of-a-kind creation. No two people resonate in the same way.

If we are fully submitted to God, it stands to reason that, in time, we will find the meaning, balance, love and purpose for which our souls hunger.

It's a process that doesn't happen overnight. But we can rest on the promise God made in Psalm 138:8a, "The LORD will perfect *that which* concerns me."

There are so many beautiful ways to paraphrase Psalm 138:8, but my favorite is from Ray Noah, "Relax! God finishes what He begins. And it's always perfect. That includes you!"

These are fundamental building blocks for every created being on earth. Some are air-breathed vocal sounds, others are percussive sounds, and still others are subtle energy frequencies.

The poetic description found in Isaiah 55:12 says, "For you shall go out in joy and be led forth in peace; the mountains and the hills before you shall break forth into singing, and all the trees of the field shall clap their hands," (ESV).

Psalm 148 tells us to:

Praise the LORD!

Praise the LORD from the heavens;

Praise Him in the heights!

Praise Him, all His angels;

Praise Him, all His hosts! Praise Him, sun and moon;

Praise Him, all you stars of light! Praise Him, you heavens of heavens, And you waters above the heavens!

Let them praise the name of the LORD,

For He commanded and they were created.

He also established them forever and ever;

He made a decree which shall not pass away.

Praise the LORD from the earth,

You great sea creatures and all the depths;

Fire and hail, snow and clouds;

Stormy wind, fulfilling His word;

Mountains and all hills;

Fruitful trees and all cedars;

Beasts and all cattle;

Creeping things and flying fowl;

 Kings of the earth and all peoples;

Princes and all judges of the earth;

Both young men and maidens;

Old men and children.

Let them praise the name of the LORD,

For His name alone is exalted;

His glory *is* above the earth and heaven.

And He has exalted the horn of His people,

The praise of all His saints— Of the children of Israel,

A people near to Him.

Praise the LORD!

Created to Sing

According to Genesis 1:26-27, we each were created in the very image of God, which means He created such a deep musical connection in us that it stands to reason that our God sings. Zephaniah 3:17 may say it best:

The LORD your God in your midst,

The Mighty One will save;

He will rejoice over you with gladness,

He will quiet *you* with His love,

He will rejoice over you with singing.

Whether anyone in your family rejoiced over you with singing, you can rest in the assurance that God does.

In Matthew 26:30, we see Jesus singing. "And when they had sung a hymn, they went out to the Mount of Olives." The singing of *Hallel* in Jewish prayer means singing the verbatim recitation of Psalm 113 through 118. Many theologians believe that Jesus and His disciples sang *Hallel* before leaving for the Mount of Olives that day.

From Genesis to Revelation, the Scriptures are rich with references to singing Deity. Many contemporary musicians have put the Psalms to music.

To know and believe in God is the best thing that
can happen in your life because He can turn what appears
to be the worst into the best. He can transform your
struggles into your learning. He can turn your suffering
into strength. He can use our failures to bring success.
– Nick Vujicic.

In Isaiah 45:12 God said, "I have made the earth, and created man on it. I— My hands— stretched out the heavens, and all their host I have commanded."

As you can see, the Bible is clear that the Father initiated creation, but the Son and Holy Spirit were the agents by whom it was made.

Over the years, I've come to realize that almost everything that can be spoken can also be sung. We see this so clearly on the opera stage.

As this concept applies to God's Word, there are obvious examples, such as singing the Psalms. In Jewish worship, the basic musical melodies and keys have been preserved and used for centuries.

Many interesting revelations are waiting to be released to us as we worship, study God's Word, pray, and operate in the gifts of the Spirit mentioned in 1 Corinthians 12:4-7. As you read this passage, remember that everything was created by sound, and that this life is voice activated.

> There are diversities of gifts, but the same Spirit. There are differences of ministries, but the same Lord. And there are diversities of activities, but it is the same God who works all in all. But the manifestation of the Spirit is given to each one for the profit *of all...*

Step Out

When you combine what we've learned about music with these amazing spiritual gifts, it becomes evident that music can deliver them in a very potent form. When music is the delivery medium, the payload contained within each gift penetrates the individual's entire being and changes the atmosphere.

Once you experience this, you'll understand that it takes faith to step out of your comfort zone and allow the Holy Spirit to give you both the words and the music. Keep in mind that it takes the same courage and faith to play the keyboard or the guitar and flow with the person singing out these amazing gifts. It is remarkable to experience the precision of the Holy Spirit. It's even more gratifying to see the enhanced and life-changing impact on the person to whom the gift is imparted.

"Where words fail, music speaks."
– Hans Christian Andersen

Music can accompany the gift of faith, gifts of healings, working of miracles, and discerning of spirits. On numerous occasions, I've seen anointed instrumentalists play over individuals and crowds, imparting spiritual downloads as they played. It's crucial to be led by the Holy Spirit to find and deliver the right combination of divine frequencies to the recipients. When the connection is made, amazing results follow.

Verbal and Visual Commands

Receiving from God always requires faith on the part of everyone involved. In this vivid account of the miracle at the Gate Beautiful, involving Peter, John, and the lame beggar, there was an additional element involved: visual contact. Peter gave a verbal instruction to the man, which was vital for this miracle to happen.

"Look on us!"

Until then, the beggar had only been focused on one thing: money. He had been placed at the Temple gate each day for years. He was operating on automatic pilot, not engaging in any way with the passers-by, except to hold out his needy hand.

When Peter said, "Look on us!" he was really saying, "Look on us because we carry your miracle inside us!"

When the beggar's eyes locked with theirs, power flowed and the faith command could be given. "In the Name of Jesus, rise up and walk." The man walked and leaped for the first time in his life. Peter's words had caused the man's focus to be on them so that their next words could put his focus where it belonged: on Jesus, the source of his miracle.

This dramatic event gave Peter the opportunity to speak to everyone in the Temple. Peter explained what had just happened. He declared that the miracle had been done through faith in the name of Jesus, even though they were the very Jews who had put Jesus to death.

Many people cross your path each day who are much like this beggar. They're desperate, begging God for someone to speak words of life over them. You carry their answer inside of you. Look in their eyes, and let God's love flow. Give them what you carry.

Going all the way with God

Think about it. Light is the offspring of sound. And light has the sonic signature of the Creator.

God haters also have a frequency, or sound. It's a toxic, violent push back against the Divine Parent and His purposes.

Darkness has a song. That song says no to every yes. It says death to all life. It says stop to every go. To every "Look to God," it says, "Look at me." To every possibility, it cries, "Impossible!"

"Impossible!"

You were born into a fallen world. You were re-born into a new world of limitless possibilities, while still residing in the toxic, fallen world. Successfully thriving in that fallen world requires a nonstop supply of sustenance from the abundance of your world of citizenship—the Kingdom of God.

It's like being an ambassador to a poor, war torn foreign country from your home country of strength, peace, stability, and plenty. Your home country doesn't require you to live at the level of the country where you are assigned. You have a continuous stream of provision coming to you from the mother country. It allows you to live at that level.

How are you supposed to have a quality, upwardly progressing life if you're always part of the problem and not part of the answer? And it's a multi-layered scenario. We're outside of God. No hope. Destined to fail, deeply embedded into death. Then, thank God, we are born again into new life in Christ Jesus. Old things have passed away, and all things have become new.

After the honeymoon period immediately following the new birth, the gravity pull from the former world begins again. We now have a decision to make, and we can jump in with a full, ever-growing intensity and an unchangeable commitment to growing in God. We can learn to utilize the supernatural endowments and provisions of our citizenship. We can live where we have all of God's ability at our full disposal, pressing into the glorious, overcoming, and prosperous life!

CHAPTER SIXTEEN

EXPAND YOUR BORDERS

"Let the word of Christ dwell in you richly in all wisdom, teaching and admonishing one another in psalms and hymns and spiritual songs, singing with grace in your hearts to the Lord," (Colossians 3:16).

Speak out to one another in psalms and hymns and spiritual songs, offering praise with voices [and instruments] and making melody with all your heart to the Lord," (Ephesians 5:19 AMPC).

Verses such as these make it clear that in the early Church, two things were happening in tandem. The power of the Holy Spirit was in operation as songs were sung both with the understanding and by the help of the Holy Spirit.

Both the expansion of the boundaries of Israel and the expansion of the boundaries of the Kingdom of God were undergirded with *SONGS*. 1 Chronicles 25 reveals that David took very seriously the worship of God in Israel, and singers and musicians were separated to the service of the Lord.

The seventh verse reveals that there were 288 skilled, dedicated worship leaders in full-time service in the Temple. It was a generational calling. All their family members were involved, generation after generation. Scriptural accounts like this one show how serious God is about music as worship, on both an individual and a corporate basis.

The Temple wasn't built and dedicated until after David's death. Yet, during his lifetime, David established an order of worship in the life of the people of God that was unprecedented. They had a hymnal of sorts—the Psalms, which they sang. The Psalms were filled with raving and boasting about

God. David understood the power of worship better than anyone else in Bible history.

Under David's leadership as a military commander and king, Israel's boundaries reached their widest dimensions. This happened simultaneously with the introduction of the largest dimensions of musical expressions in worship that the people of Israel ever reached. Those two things didn't happen by accident; they were planned by God.

The extension of the Kingdom of God was being manifest at that stage of redemptive history. It happened under the leadership of a ruler who'd been told that the Redeemer would come through his family line. That promise had been given to David, the son of Jesse, and the king of Israel. God moved in his heart in such a dynamic way that worship became a part of the lives of God's people like it had never been before. To this day, Jesus is referred to as the Son of David. As the worship expanded, so did the national boundaries.

We are only beginning to glimpse the power of the priority to worship. The presence of the Lord is always welcomed by worship through song, glorifying His name. The expansion of those boundaries through worship also destroyed the powers of hell to resist it. The anointed, worshiping Covenant family of God marched like an army in triumphant song and demonstration.

What they experienced under David's leadership of worship has seldom been seen in the lives of believers today. Many of us are new in Christ. Others have grown up in the church and walked with the Lord for many years. Regardless of the duration of time involved, there is a great deal of evidence that most people have had little understanding of all the reasons for which God gave us song. Today, we're coming into a fresh appreciation not only of the joy of music, but of its power in every circumstance in our lives.

It was said of first-century Christians, "They are turning the world upside down," (Acts 17:6). Accompanying that supernatural power was *SONG*.

Woven into the fabric of the early Church were triumphant, overcoming, victorious Spirit-filled songs. They bridged the ages, reaching back in time to pick up the Psalms, while adding new melodies, new developments, and new applications. We would see miraculous changes in our individual lives and our corporate services today if we brought that same flow of the Holy Spirit into our worship.

What happened could be summed up in 1 Chronicles 25:7: People were being instructed in the song of the Lord. They were being taught to enter into a dynamic expansion of worship. Imagine the difference in families today if our children had been instructed in the song of the Lord. Living that way, the dimensions of God's plan for our lives might be pushed to their maximum boundaries.

Music is the mediator between the life of
the senses and the life of the spirit.
– Ludwig von Beethoven 1770-1827

Songs have been given to us as more than just a point of participation when believers get together. Songs are more than just to lift our hearts through inspiration. They're more than a preliminary activity prior to the "important part" of a church service.

They're more than mere performance.

They're more than just aesthetics.

The song of the Lord is not only to glorify His name. It brings power to push forward the boundaries of God's plan.

I've walked into places where there was another spirit at work. Those places felt suffocating with stifling oppression. Buildings, places of business, schools, restaurants, and homes will reflect the ruling spirit.

For instance, in 1981, I traveled to South Africa with a group of missionaries. We flew in a bush plane to a village near the border between Mozambique and South Africa, not far from the Kruger National Park. We wanted to hold an outreach there, but the ruling authority in that village was the witch doctor. We took him big bags of maize, what we call corn, as a gift.

About seven of us went to his compound, which was a mud house with a circular fence around it to keep animals out. There was no grass, just dirt. His house was painted with images of demon spirits. I was last in line when we entered his yard, and I saw a woman leaning against the fence post. Naked from the waist up, she wore some sort of wrap below her waist.

Using a mallet, she beat a slow cadence on a big drum. I dropped behind as the others went inside. Her eyes were rolled back in her head, and I knew she was in a trance. The pungent odor led me to believe she'd been there for days. I stood beside her and in a soft voice, sang "Amazing Grace" into her ear. I sang to the rhythm of her drum.

"Amazing grace, how sweet the sound that saved a wretch…"

That's as far as I got. The moment I sang the word "wretch," her eyes rolled back to their proper position in her head. She threw the drum aside and screamed the most demonized scream I'd ever heard. Still holding the drum mallet, she began to chase me around the compound. She kept coming. She was gaining on me.

I stopped in my tracks and turned to face her.

Holding my hand in the shape of a gun, I pretended to shoot her. At the same time, I screamed, *"Jesus!"*

When I yelled the name of Jesus, it was as though she'd been shot. That name knocked her off her feet and she flew backward eight or ten feet.

I walked to her and stood over her. "Jesus," I said, "is Lord."

She stuttered in a weak voice. "Ye..Ye…yes. Ye…yes."

> I went inside the witch doctor's house, and she was gone when we came back outside.

> I've always believed that she was born again when she agreed that yes, Jesus is Lord.

That's the power of song when faced with demonic forces.

"Amazing Grace" was written in 1791 by John Newton, a British captain in the slave trade. He and other sick men had been unloaded onto the West Indies and left to die. Newton recovered, and a woman missionary led him to the Lord. He was rescued by a passing ship and returned to England

He'd spent a lot of his former life in pubs. Now a Christian, he took the melody from one of the pub songs and wrote "Amazing Grace" lyrics to go with it. Millions of lives have been changed by God through this famous song.

On the Wings of a Song

Here are some of our greatest inspirations to worship:

> His excellent greatness (Psalm150:2).

> The beauty of the Lord's love for us.

> The magnificence of His grace in Jesus.

> The tenderness of His embrace toward us.

> His forgiveness.

> His healing touch.

> How He has blessed us in our lives.

> His faithfulness to His Word.

> The authority we have as believers.

> His protection from calamity.

When we worship God for these things, oppression lifts. There's a sense of reprieve from pressure, and the Lord's healing presence arrives on the scene.

This life of worship, borne on the wings of SONG, is not something that works because you have the richest understanding or the keenest discernment. It works because you appropriate the privilege of the power of song upon the lips of God's people as they praise.

When we live in that place, a new flow of life and liberty manifests in our lives. That's what God desires for each of us. The avenue of song is a quick pathway to that experience.

Music…will help dissolve your perplexities and purify your character and sensibilities, and in time of sorrow, will keep a fountain of joy alive in you.
– Dietrich Bonhoeffer

Sing, O Barren

I am indebted to my mentor and friend, Pastor Jack Hayford, for his vital input into my walk with Jesus for many decades, especially as it relates to worship. We have many teachers, but few fathers.

Among the ancient people of Israel, there was no greater stigma for a married woman than to be unable to bear children. Today, a barren woman might be discouraged, but she would never be mocked by society. No one would point a finger at her and say that God didn't love her.

Childless women felt shame and rejection. They felt inadequate. In the face of all that rejection, can you imagine the prophet saying, "Sing, O barren...?" But that's just what he did.

"Sing, O barren,

Thou that didst not bear.

Break forth into singing, and cry aloud, You *who* have not labored with child!

For more *are* the children of the desolate

Than the children of the married woman," says the LORD.

"Enlarge the place of your tent,

And let them stretch out the curtains of your dwellings;

Do not spare;

Lengthen your cords,

And strengthen your stakes.

For you shall expand to the right and to the left,

And your descendants will inherit the nations,

And make the desolate cities inhabited.

"Do not fear, for you will not be ashamed;

Neither be disgraced, for you will not be put to shame;

For you will forget the shame of your youth,

And will not remember the reproach of your widowhood anymore," (Isaiah 54:1-4).

At some point, we've all experienced points of barrenness in our lives – times when you've been standing for years for the fruit of your prayers to manifest. So deep is the blindness, the addiction, the sin, or the tormenting doubt in that family member that you wonder if he or she will *ever* turn to Jesus.

How often have we, like barren women, hoped for something to be born in our lives? Something that would fulfill a dream, a desire, or a goal.

The world is full of people who aspire to things that aren't wrong or unspiritual. We may long for a successful business, healthy relationships, and happy experiences. We might lie awake at night wondering why the thing we've longed for hasn't manifested. We stand in faith, speak His promises, and pray. We try not to speak out words of unbelief or fear. We feel fatigued and discouraged. It's not wrong to ask God, "Why do I feel this way? I'm bewildered."

How do we treat such situations? God told us in Isaiah 54. We *sing* over all the barren places of our lives.

One woman told us that she'd suffered from a serious weight problem and was depressed at the barrenness she found in every diet that she pursued. "The Holy Spirit took me to Isaiah 54 and made it alive to me," she said. "I took it to heart and began to sing over my weight problem. I now stand before you 60 pounds lighter. My health is under control." Worship drives out barrenness! It brings new life.

Song is an instrument of breakthrough, deliverance, and victory.

The psalmist sang it this way, "You *are* my hiding place; You shall preserve me from trouble; You shall surround me with songs of deliverance," (Psalm 32:7).

A woman who'd suffered from a chronic physical problem had been prayed for by many people, but she was no better. She grew worse, having no results. A pastor gathered other believers and they circled her. They stood around her and sang and worshiped. They literally placed her in a worship crossfire, as we have discussed earlier in Chapter 13.

A few days later, she got documented proof that she had been made whole. The power of song brings worship, breakthrough and victory.

SONGS OF DELIVERANCE

In Acts, chapter 16, Paul and Silas went to Philippi where they cast a spirit of divination out of a young girl. Knowing they couldn't make any more money from her fortune telling, the girl's masters had Paul and Silas beaten and thrown in prison.

> Then the multitude rose up together against them; and the magistrates tore off their clothes and commanded *them* to be beaten with rods. And when they had laid many stripes on them, they threw *them* into prison, commanding the jailer to keep them securely. Having received such a charge, he put them into the inner prison and fastened their feet in stocks.
>
> But at midnight Paul and Silas were praying and singing hymns to God, and the prisoners were listening to them. Suddenly there was a great earthquake, so that the foundations of the prison were shaken; and immediately all the doors were opened and everyone's chains were loosed (Acts 16:22-26).

What a miracle! Songs of praise and worship caused an earthquake! The jailer and prisoners fell on their knees and called on Jesus to save them. The power of song led to Paul and Silas' deliverance from jail, the salvation of a whole family, the establishment of a local church, and the spread of the Gospel to the whole world.

The Gospel was breaking into a new continent in Philippi. There were new principalities, powers, and religious spirits to deal with. The trip to Philippi took the Gospel through Greece, to Europe, and from Europe to us.

Just think, it all started with a song.

This is for you, today. The Holy Spirit wants us to be instructed anew in the song of the Lord. Just as Israel's boundaries were expanded, your boundaries will be expanded. The Lord is calling you in your own personal life to dimensions of possibility you've never known. SONG will open the pathway into that. Have the simplicity of heart to worship with childlike abandon in candid, simple openness before the Lord. That attitude says, "Lord, I *will* worship you in spirit and in truth with song. I'll sing in the spirit and with the understanding. I will open my heart and lift my voice to you. You are worthy of my praise, and *SONG* will become my deliverance and breakthrough.

Praise in the face of tragedy and barrenness is truly one of the highest forms of faith. Regardless of the circumstances around me, I will sing your praises and deliverance will come.

CHAPTER SEVENTEEN

HIGH ALTITUDE
WITH THE MOST HIGH

The flight from Sydney to Rome was long, with a quick stop in Jakarta. The early part of the journey took us over Australia's northeastern archipelago, then westward over southern Borneo, Sumatra, and Myanmar. It was still daytime, and the flight was smooth and quiet. In silence, I prayed for the island nations below me, occasionally singing my prayers under my breath.

Earlier, I'd seen two Muslim businessmen roll out their janamaz, or prayer rugs, turn toward Mecca and bow, praying in Arabic. After a few minutes, they rolled up their mats, put them in the overhead, and went back to working on their laptops.

Lunch was served and lunch trays collected. The love of God for those two men touched my heart, and as I looked out the window, I quietly prayed for them.

In a moment, I sensed someone standing to my left in the aisle. Looking up, I saw that it was those two businessmen. We exchanged pleasantries, and one of them said, "We were in our seats during lunch talking about you. We don't quite know how to describe what we were feeling, but..." There was a long pause before he continued. "You are good, aren't you?"

They were so sincere and precious. They wanted to know what was different about me. I hadn't spoken to them or looked back in their direction, yet something drew them to me. The seat on my left was empty, so I invited one of them to sit down. The other one stood by his side. First, I complimented them on their perception and sensitivity to spiritual things.

Over the next hour and a half, I explained to them what they were sensing about me. I made it clear that it was the goodness of the Savior Jesus that was resident in me.

Just then, we were ordered back to our seats for our approach into Soekarno-Hatta International Airport in Jakarta. Instead of going to their seats, they stayed where they were, not moving even though we were descending. I asked if they had any needs that I could pray about.

They each had family members with challenges in several areas. We held hands, and I prayed. As I did, the power of God enveloped them, and they both began crying. I asked if they would like to receive Jesus. They wiped their eyes and looked around. Then they politely declined.

I assured them that they could pray anytime, anywhere to receive Jesus. They were both smiling and glowing as we deplaned. We continued our conversation as we walked up the jetway. I urged them to find a strong Christian congregation to help answer any questions.

Indonesia is the largest Muslim country on earth. It was a deep and serious decision the two men were dealing with. I believe they prayed in their hearts on the plane with me and would seek out the next step to beginning their walk with Jesus.

What happened at altitude that day? I believe that as I worshiped the Father and Son, an atmosphere of glory was created around me. The Holy Spirit began to draw those men to Jesus. I believe that what He started that day, He continued after they deplaned. As they shook hands with me and disappeared into the dense crowd, I heard the Lord say, *"I've got them! And 17 other people around you heard every word you said. I'm working on them, too!"*

The Key Element is Song

I've found that there are three common characteristics of people who are consistent and successful about receiving from the Lord.

1. They feed themselves on the ultimate spiritual nourishment, the Word of God.

2. They receive and believe every revelation of truth and act in a way that reveals their faith in that Word.

3. They speak and sing words of faith in their own lives.

There is a spiritual key that combines all three characteristics of a person who receives well from the Lord. That key element is singing a new song.

- It accelerates spiritual development.

- It increases their capacity to draw from every attribute of God.

- It increases their capacity to secure the promises of God.

- It expands their dominion of joy and happiness.

If I were a spiritual doctor, I'd advise you to open your mouth and sing every day. This will open the door even wider for His glory to fill your life. What would you sing?

- Sing a fresh expression of new life in Christ.

- Sing about being clothed with His righteousness.

- Sing about His goodness.

- Sing about Who He is.

- Sing about what He has done for you.

- Sing about how His mercies are new every morning.

- Sing His praises and your thanksgiving.

- Sing your love for Him.

- Sing about His love for you.

- Then, get quiet and listen to His reply.

How powerful is singing? How powerful is putting a melody to anointed words? Singing worship to God is powerful enough for the book of Psalms alone to mention it more than 70 times.

Here are five verses from Psalm 33:

> Sing joyfully to the LORD, you righteous; it is fitting for the upright to praise him.
>
> Praise the LORD with the harp; make music to him on the ten-stringed lyre. Sing to him a new song; play skillfully, and shout for joy. For the word of the LORD is right and true; he is faithful in all he does. The LORD loves righteousness and justice; the earth is full of his unfailing love (Psalm 33:1-5 NIV).

God Himself has put a new song in your mouth. Musically speaking, accept the grace from God when He gives you the very song you need to worship Him. It might be a song already written or a spontaneous expression right out of your heart.

You might be thinking, *I'd like to sing a spontaneous song to God and into my situation, but I've never done that before. I can't even carry a tune."*

If you will open your mouth by faith, that song will come out, not only helping you but also giving God greater access to you. Just sing the truth about God, the absolute dependability of His promises, the certainty of His love, and the precision of His timing regarding your life. Your song will be beautiful in Gods ears, however it may sound to you. You might be the one God uses to write another "Amazing Grace" or "How Great is Our God"!

Learn to join forces with the forces of Heaven.
– Len Mink

Climbing Jacob's Ladder

In Genesis 28, Jacob's ladder shows us angels ascending and descending from Heaven. It helps us understand a spiritual reality. Words and music are our ladder to ascend into the presence of God. Words also bring the angels down into our specific areas of need. That ladder is Jesus Himself, the Living Word. As we sing, speak, think, and focus on the certainty of God's promises, His Word manifests.

We're told this in Hebrews 4:12, "For the word of God is quick, and powerful, and sharper than any two-edged sword, piercing even to the dividing asunder of soul and spirit, and of the joints and marrow, and is a discerner of the thoughts and intents of the heart."

In Rick Renner's book, *Sparkling Gems from the Greek,* we're told that the Greek word for two-edged is *distomas,* or twice spoken. *Di* means two, and *stomas* means opening or mouth. The Word of God was first spoken by God so that it could be written down by men – and spoken again by us. Our speaking is the second edge.

The dark side trembles if even a small child who trusts God speaks or sings God's Word. A recent news story illustrates the power of divine song.

A 10-year-old Boy Who Was Kidnapped Sang His Way to Freedom. A gospel song saved a 10-year-old Atlanta boy from his kidnapper. Willie Myrick said he was in his front yard and bent down to pick up money when somebody grabbed him and threw him in a car.

"He told me he didn't want to hear a word from me," Myrick said. That's when Myrick began to sing a gospel song called "Every Praise." The kidnapper started cursing and repeatedly told Myrick to shut up, but he wouldn't. He sang the song for about three hours until the kidnapper let him out of the car.

The little boy ran to a nearby home and asked the resident to call his guardian. Myrick recently got to meet "Every Praise" gospel singer Hezekiah Walker, and they sang the song together.[21]

Because Willie knew what to do, God showed up and set him free. God did what He promised in Isaiah 54:17, "No weapon formed against you shall prosper...."

Willie's freedom came on the wings of a song!

Passionate Praise

The Bible records many instances where God's people celebrated their victories by singing and dancing. For instance, Exodus chapter 15 records a song sung by the children of Israel to God. Moses, Miriam, and Aaron were all highly developed psalmists. This scripture is a song, a musical and lyrical outward passionate explosion of praise to God for the miracle at the Red Sea.

"I will sing to the LORD,

For He has triumphed gloriously!

The horse and its rider

He has thrown into the sea!

The LORD *is* my strength and song,

And He has become my salvation;

He *is* my God, and I will praise Him;

My father's God, and I will exalt Him.

The LORD *is* a man of war;

The LORD *is* His name.

Pharaoh's chariots and his army He has cast into the sea;

His chosen captains also are drowned in the Red Sea.

The depths have covered them;

They sank to the bottom like a stone.

Your right hand, O LORD, has become glorious in power;

Your right hand, O LORD, has dashed the enemy in pieces,"

(Exodus 15:1-6).

God has put into the hearts of His children a deep desire to recall and recite history, victories, important events, and cultural monuments. They are there to undergird the present and direct our footsteps into the future. Many cultures have a process of teaching about past events that is not only verbal, but includes such visual aids as acting or dancing to depict the details of what happened.

By far, the most common method of revisiting historical happenings is through song. What a massive victory this was for the Israelites! An entire civilization had been supernaturally preserved by this epic miracle of God.

The Red Sea marvel was cemented into history when Miriam grabbed her timbrel as she danced and sang along with Moses. In the 40 years it took them to reach Jericho, their first and biggest hurdle had been in Canaan. It seems the story of the Red Sea miracle with the destruction of the Egyptian assailants had reached the ears of all of Canaan. It's possible that the song they first sang on the western shore of the Red Sea "took over" in the Canaanite culture. It might have become number one on the charts as the top hit in Canaan, striking fear into the hearts of all the citizens of Jericho.

The more you sing, the more His power will flow. The more you worship in song, the stronger you get. The more often you give wings to song in passionate praise, the more healing will flow and the more prophetic words will be delivered from Heaven. Wisdom, peace, and prosperity will show up on the scene.

The new song flowing out of your heart is enabled by the Holy Spirit. You will radiate the presence of God because your worship has become a conduit through which the power and love of God can flow to desperate people. An atmosphere charged with the presence of God is one of the strongest tools of evangelism in existence.

CHAPTER EIGHTEEN

DEVELOPING SPIRITUAL WORSHIP BEYOND THE VEIL

As we study the Word of God regarding worship, it becomes clear that God is drawing us closer to Himself. He's always seeking avenues of blessing for His beloved children. He desires access for His provision to flow with unhindered expressions of His grace and love. Let's look back into the history of worship and work our way forward to the present.

Using Old Testament patterns of worship, we find ourselves moving from the outer gates of the tabernacle to the inner courts of the Temple. This inner court was beyond the veil that separated the Holy Place from the Holy of Holies. This is a picture of progressive praise and worship that keeps advancing deeper into the very manifest presence of God. In the Holy of Holies, there was nothing artificial, just His light. There was no outside influence of humanity— only the magnificent presence of God.

Looking further back in history, we find that there was no evidence of music being used in worshiping God during the time when Moses led the children of Israel in the wilderness. They offered a lot of prayer and sacrifices, but no music. Miriam's song of victory at the Red Sea crossing was the last mention of song in this forty year period.

There were songs written by Miriam, Aaron, and Moses, as well as others. However, none of these were used in worship in the tent tabernacle in the wilderness. That didn't change until David carried the Ark of the Covenant up to Jerusalem, also known as the City of David.

There was a very demonstrative breaking free from normal traditions of the past, a fresh new liberty and diverse manifestations of praise and worship. Under David, they worshiped with shouting, dancing, singing, leaping, and playing various musical instruments.

As I've noted before, it's interesting that Israel's geographical expansion and their growing military conquests were proportional to the development of their expression of worship to God. David's personal life of worship was the seedbed of Israel's growth in worship.

David's son, Solomon, built the Temple in Jerusalem and continued his father's precepts in worship by establishing guidelines that would ensure their perpetuation. At the opening of the Temple, David's Psalm 30 was used as the song of dedication. David had wanted God to be glorified and all the attention drawn to Him. They did away with anything that would detract from the focus on God.

Today, the same reason must prevail for creating guidelines, rules, and standards regarding our worship. During my years as a worship leader, I've gained some insight into this crucial facet of our lives before God.

Through the years of countless musical genre changes, as well as special effects and synthetic and robotic presentations, there remain a few foundational keys and precepts that will take us deeper into worship.

You may be a music minister, a worship team member, a musician, someone who just likes to worship, or even someone who doesn't sense any musical expression at all. Regardless of where you are, instruction on this subject will prove to be invaluable.

How we worship is so important to God that Jesus said His Father was always looking for those who would worship the right way. We see an example of this in John 4:19-26 when the Samaritan woman went to Jacob's well.

The woman said to Him, "Sir, I perceive that You are a prophet. Our fathers worshiped on this mountain, and you Jews say that in Jerusalem is the place where one ought to worship."

Jesus said to her, "Woman, believe Me, the hour is coming when you will neither on this mountain, nor in Jerusalem, worship the Father. You worship what you do not know; we know what we worship, for salvation is of the Jews. But the hour is coming, and now is, when the true worshipers will worship the Father in spirit and truth; for the Father is seeking such to worship Him. God *is* Spirit, and those who worship Him must worship in spirit and truth."

The woman said to Him, "I know that Messiah is coming" (who is called Christ). When He comes, He will tell us all things. Jesus said to her, "I who speak to you am *He*."

Can you imagine the impact this must have had on that woman? She went to the well just to fill her water pot. Jesus was there, thirsty and dry. He asked her for a drink of water. The woman was bold and took the initiative in the conversation. Recognizing His clothing, she took a trip down a time-worn religious pathway.

Jesus told her that the time was coming when everyone would worship in spirit and in truth. Anytime places or positions of the body take precedence over the attitude of the heart, we're missing the point. So many worship services have become nothing more than a performance for the people. Tragically, the people perform back to the pulpit in a well choreographed religious exhibition. There needs to be room for the Holy Spirit to lift the praise to a higher level.

Worship in the Spirit with the Right Attitude of Heart

We worship with our spirit, not just our flesh. Onstage at events, I have a bird's eye view of the audience. From where I stand, I can take a rather accurate reading of the level of worship. Much of the time, especially in the American church, people are just going through the motions, detached, thinking about something else.

They're missing an encounter with God.

If we worship with our whole being—spirit, soul, and body—we connect with covenant provision, revelation knowledge, advancement, and favor.

That's what King David established that was so revolutionary. He worshiped God with his whole being, not just with the words of his mouth. He leapt, danced, and clapped before the Lord. He had all kinds of instruments used in worship: strings, brass, percussion, vocal, and whatever else he could find.

It's crucial to have the right attitude of heart, but that alone isn't enough. We need to worship God's way—*in total reverence and respect*, yet with full awareness of the love between Father and child.

There is a certain way to approach an awesome God. Cain and Abel learned that lesson well. They found that they had to follow God's prescribed plan for worship. Not just any old sloppy, thrown together, self-manufactured thing would work.

Worshipping the Lord in truth means worshiping Him according to God's Word. It means using the supernatural frequencies of God found in the Word to form rivers of praise. It means singing the Word, sending His very words back to Him as a form of worship.

When we do this, we worship by faith.

According to Hebrews 11:1, things done in faith have substance and tangibility. Without faith it's impossible to please the Father (Hebrews 11:6).

As mentioned in John 4:24, God is *still* looking for those who will worship Him in Spirit and in truth.

The Greek definition of worship is the word *proskuneo*, which means to prostrate oneself in homage. Spiritual worship is all about bringing pleasure to the heart of our Master. Its focus should always be, "What can I do to bring pleasure and blessing to the Lord, and how can I express my thanks to Him for all He has done for me?"

I've been deliberate about this in my own personal worship. Sometimes, I place an empty chair in the middle of the room and picture Jesus sitting there. Then I walk around the chair, finding words, songs, phrases and physical gestures to express my love and gratitude to Him. It soon becomes so tangible that worship flows unhindered as His presence fills the room.

Have you ever wondered why Jesus spent so much time at the home of Martha, Mary, and Lazarus? I believe it's because both His deity and His humanity were recognized and ministered to there. When that happens, you can get your brother raised from the dead!

Scriptural worship is a symbiotic give-and-take experience. You've got to know that you'll never be pushed away. There is an intimate relationship, both partners giving to each other.

The Bible assures us that God rewards those who diligently seek Him (Hebrews 11:6).

He's nothing like a cold, distant, unaffectionate father on earth. He rewards you on approach.

Psychologists tell us that basic trust is developed in a human being one way and one way only: through human touch. Scriptural worship is touching God and allowing Him to touch you. There is both initiation and response. God doesn't sit there like a statue demanding, "Come to me!"

The number one cop-out phrase for most Christians concerning worship is, "That's not my personality." That might be why you don't experience breakthroughs and your life is boring. You're stuck! Only *you* can break *you* free.

To understand true worship, we must step out of that self-focused zone of comfortable predictability into the arena of faith. As we do, we'll find God rushing to meet us with joy unspeakable and full of glory.

Worship Wisdom

Real, authentic worship is godly. It's not coarse, acting out to fill some empty cavern of rejection and get its own needs met. Be very careful about use of banners, free dance, tambourines and instruments being played in the congregation. Yes, there are scriptures that mention most of those things. However, very few first-time visitors understand losing their hearing from a surprise shofar blast. Leaders should lead their worship services to be uplifting and welcoming, not something visitors need counseling to recover from.

Over several decades of ministry, in thousands of different settings, I've seen countless numbers of people come into church and be treated poorly, embarrassed, ignored, or even abused. Pastors need to lay down rules of conduct. Ushers need to be trained in hospitality and security. Things that are too distracting and only call attention to individuals and not to God need to be managed. The congregation and visitors need to be protected. The church must not fail them. It's sad to say, but when a Christian leader fails to control things in the house of God, it's almost always about money. He or she doesn't want to offend any donors. "Feed my sheep," however, also means "Protect my sheep."

However, there is good news. There is a rising tide of well balanced, loving, no-nonsense leadership who teach the strong Word of God. They encourage the gifts of the Spirit and work tirelessly to see people's needs met. Worshiping God's way is a major ingredient in making this a living reality.

Make sure that you're a blessing, not a liability. True worshipers usher in the love of God, and people are lifted and healed.

Don't forget that Lucifer was an anointed angel, created by God and placed in charge of Heaven's music. His beauty sparkled through Heaven. He had internal instruments embedded in him. He got puffed up with pride and announced in Isaiah 14:14, "I will be like the Most High."

God banished him from Heaven because he sought to exalt himself and his music ministry above all else. Have you ever known anyone like that? I call it L.A.M.S., or Look At Me Syndrome.

What does this say to us who are the worship leaders of today? Stay humble, with Kingdom-of-God motives. Stay teachable. Remain pure regarding the Word of God. Stay pure financially and sexually, and never draw back from those in authority over you. Never draw back from God's direction.

Any ministry that becomes a controlling empire is not from God. A voice or instrument that insists on being heard above all others is a voice or instrument that is not flowing in unity.

I've been a guest minister several times at a church where a very gifted guitar player, known for his great ability, refused to play on the church worship team unless he was given solos on nearly every song. When the weak leadership began allowing this, the anointing flew out the door. Many people also left with their spiritual supply and financial support.

God has musical abilities so far beyond our natural
thoughts that it's essential for us to be tuned in to Him.
– Len Mink

The pastoral leadership may not have the awe-inspiring insight and revelation you have regarding music and worship, but they are still the leaders. Statistically, musicians have caused more church splits than anyone else.

A musician who wants to control others – the sound, the lighting, the song selection, order of worship, or time boundaries – is setting himself up for a major fall. Musicians who gather a disgruntled following to agree with them need to get on their faces and repent.

The point here is that God doesn't commit to talent. He doesn't commit to revelation. He doesn't commit to power. God commits to character.

If you can't pass the character test, God can't trust you with leadership, money, buildings, revelation, information, or blessing past your last act of pride or disobedience.

One-third of the angels followed Lucifer to the pit. It *is* possible to get a following and leave with a following. And it *is* possible to lead that following straight to the pit. Statistically, rebellious worship leaders who break off into a new group and go elsewhere have a short honeymoon period before they find themselves on the rocks. Their work is closed within a short period of time, leaving sheep bleeding in the ditches begging God for a real shepherd.

Jesus said, "I beheld Satan as lightning fall from heaven," (Luke 10:18)

Lightning is an electric discharge from cloud to cloud or from cloud to earth. The discharge is normally initiated by negative polarity. I think we would be accurate in saying that when Satan was banished from Heaven, there was a negative discharge resulting in a monumental display of lightning.

Progressive Praise

God has musical abilities so far beyond our natural thoughts that it's essential for us to be tuned in to Him. For example, it's vital that our personal worship start at home before the corporate worship begins at church. Come early to the house of God. Don't arrive just as the service starts. Never arrive after praise and worship is over. Value the house of God.

For years, I've heard people who consider themselves to be super-spiritual say, "I just come for the Word, the meat!" Those people are filled with spiritual pride and self-focus; and they're probably not tithers, either!

When you go to church, expect a miracle. Buy a $25 watch and be early, praying, believing, and helping by getting into the flow. Don't argue on the way to church. Get your mind off yourself and your problems. Worship allows better absorption and deeper understanding of the Word of God. It assures that the information you're given will morph into revelation.

Praise and worship aren't optional entertainment. Praise and sacred surrender to God should never be viewed as filler before the important stuff.

God's arm is always extended toward you for good. Psalm 98:1 says, "O sing unto the LORD a new song; for he hath done marvelous things: his right hand and his holy arm hath gotten him the victory."

Let's take another look at Psalm 98:1-4:

> Oh, sing to the LORD a new song!
>
> For He has done marvelous things;
>
> His right hand and His holy arm have gained Him the victory.
>
> The LORD has made known His salvation;
>
> His righteousness He has revealed in the sight of the nations.
>
> He has remembered His mercy and His faithfulness to the house of Israel;
>
> All the ends of the earth have seen the salvation of our God.
>
> Shout joyfully to the LORD, all the earth;
>
> Break forth in song, rejoice, and sing praises.

The first verse tells us to sing to the Lord a new song. The word new in Hebrew is *hadash,* which means new, fresh, repaired, and rebuilt.

I think it is vital that we sing Him a new song because the music of *this* world is broken.

When Satan was kicked out of Heaven, he took his music with him. He corrupted and twisted it. Twisted means something is wicked. It's where we get words like wicker, wick, and wiccan. His music was an extension of his influence, and it became freakish and distorted.

That's why in a lot of the music you hear today, there's a dissonance, a clash among musical notes which disagree in sound. There's no harmonious flow, no unity. It's jarring, and it disrupts peace. It broadcasts the frequencies of the flesh, and the flesh responds. There are a lot of disjointed sounds, each telling the listener, "Follow me. Copy me. Sound like me." The music sells deception to uninformed people.

God's music is fresh, upbeat, creative, and multifaceted. It uplifts those hearing it and points to Jesus. It's filled with God's love and light. The Holy Spirit is always at work within it.

Having come from a show-business background, I can tell you that there was nothing there that filled my soul. Yet I'm amazed at the questions I hear from Christian song writers, musicians and singers. "How far can we go? How close can we get to the world's music and still be classified as Christian?"

Finding Jesus

When I found Jesus, I found what my soul hungered for. I departed show business so that I could express what music was intended to do, which is to glorify God. It pains me to see so many young singers on TV talent shows reveal that their musical roots were in the church, yet they seem to have taken a page out of Lucifer's playbook, "Look at me!"

The question *should* be, "How can the world become more like us?" But if we act goofy and out of touch with the needs of the world, people will have no reason to be like us.

What typifies a song as Christian? Is it just the lyrics? Is it the style of musical arrangement or an identifiable genre flavor?

Should Christian artists have a distinctive look or, for the sake of relevancy, look like they just got blown in by a hurricane—grubby and cool?

These are all legitimate questions. They are a cry for guidelines, not legalism.

What is the best way to draw the world to Christ without compromising His message? This requires a supernatural work of the Spirit of God in our worship.

We can't afford to ignore Psalm 98, which says that it's time for a new song, a new freshness, and new music indwelt with God's notes and lyrics. We need music that has been rebuilt, repaired, and born again.

Don't copy the toxic songs of the world.

We don't need gimmicks or clever hooks.

We just need Him.

According to Psalm 98:4, we can have joyful, fun music in which we rejoice. There's no end to God's ability and desire to impart new revelation regarding worship. There are musical expressions of worship so fresh and supernatural that they reveal facets of God that have never been seen.

It's all there, in the Spirit, waiting to be discovered by those who will not compromise.

While it's easy to copy the world's music, it takes pressing into the heart of God to get the new songs. That journey begins and ends with this: How hungry are we to find and flow in this new, supernatural genesis of divine frequencies?

Heaven is pregnant with the sounds and notes that will usher in the mighty presence of God. The new sound says, "I hunger and thirst to be in closer proximity and intimacy with my Savior."

Sometimes we're so wrapped up in the work of the Lord that we forget the Lord of the work. Our worship should be done with excellence, with good sound and light, and be well-rehearsed and honoring to God. However, we must purpose to move away from giving top priority to props and technical delivery systems and their complexities.

Switch off the technical details. Let the people assigned to those jobs do them, so that you as a leader can take the congregation into the presence of God. People want to *feel* the presence of God. They're changed by that encounter.

Most people aren't aware of this, but there is a marked difference between a *worship leader* and a *lead worshiper*. A worship leader is one who presents, displays or performs worship material before the people. If people get anything out of it, it's because *they* choose to enter worship. Sometimes a worship service is merely a dazzling display of sounds, lights, superb vocals, special effects, and *wow* factors, devoid of the anointing (the tangible presence of God).

A lead worshiper, on the other hand, is someone who has been alone with God behind closed doors. They've gone deep, using their personal faith to connect with Him. They don't perform. They *impart*. People need authenticity. They suffer when worship is synthetic.

I'll never forget an experience I had years ago in a tiny country church. I was the guest minster for that service. Before I was to share, the pastor invited a precious little grandma to bring her guitar and sing one song while the offering was being received.

Her guitar was missing a string. She wore a plain dress, and she was a bit uncomfortable in front of a group of people. After a few long seconds of hesitancy, she strummed a chord and opened her mouth in song.

A tsunami of glory hit that place and nearly knocked us to the floor. We all joined her, and before we knew it, time had passed and the service was over. People had been born again, healed, and filled with the Holy Spirit. There had been too many miracles to count.

God has such a great sense of humor. I never got to minister. A man came up to me at the end of the service and shook my hand. "Thank you for coming, brother. That was the best service I've ever attended."

She was a lead worshiper.

Let's return to the words of Paul. "What is *the conclusion* then? I will pray with the spirit, and I will also pray with the understanding. I will sing with the spirit, and I will also sing with the understanding," (1 Corinthians 14:15).

This verse describes a flowing back and forth in spiritual song. It creates an atmosphere of glory where God can express His love as our praise builds a river flowing out of God's supply to a needy world.

As we follow this pattern, the windows of Heaven will open over us and pour out signs, wonders, and miracles.

Beyond the curtain.

Beyond the veil.

Into a continual manifestation of the presence of God.

CHAPTER NINETEEN

THE SUPERNATURAL
SONIC WEAPON

There were no words spoken or sung as the Israelites marched in cadence around Jericho. Not a shout. Not a battle cry.

Jericho was terrifying, a formidable fortress.

The first tier of the stone wall stood 12 to 15 feet tall on top of an earthen embankment. Atop the stone retaining wall, stood another wall made of mud bricks. It was about six feet thick and 20 to 26 feet high. Together, the two walls combined formed a wall 32 to 41 feet tall.[22]

It seemed impenetrable.

The Israelites must have looked like grasshoppers to those watching from inside the fortress. They must have felt like ants.

The Israelites had to dispossess the Canaanites and take the city of Jericho in order to occupy the promised land. It was their first big challenge after the miracle at the Red Sea.

Would God rescue them again?

If they could take Jericho, they could defeat anything.

The fall of Jericho was one of the most astounding miracles in the Bible, and it bears taking a closer look. In Joshua 5:13-15, the children of Israel were camped near Jericho. "And it came to pass, when Joshua was by Jericho, that he lifted his eyes and looked, and behold, a Man stood opposite him with His sword drawn in His hand."

And Joshua went to Him and said to Him, "*Are* You for us or for our adversaries?" So He said, "No, but *as* Commander of the army of the LORD I have now come." And Joshua fell on his face to the earth and worshiped, and said to Him, "What does my Lord say to His servant?" Then the Commander of the LORD's army said to Joshua, "Take your sandal off your foot, for the place where you stand *is* holy." And Joshua did so.

When the Man identified Himself as the commander of the Lord's army, Joshua knew this was not an angel, but God Himself. It might have been the pre-incarnate Jesus (Micah 5:2; Genesis 18:16-33; Genesis 32:24-30; Judges 13:1-23).

Joshua was familiar with the story of the burning bush in Exodus 3. He knew that the voice was the one heard by Moses from the bush.

Obeying the Lord's command, Joshua took off his shoes. God had shown up to tell him how to take Jericho. Look at what happened in Joshua 6:1-5:

> Now Jericho was securely shut up because of the children of Israel; none went out, and none came in. And the LORD said to Joshua: "See! I have given Jericho into your hand, its king, *and* the mighty men of valor. You shall march around the city, all *you* men of war; you shall go all around the city once. This you shall do six days. And seven priests shall bear seven trumpets of rams' horns before the ark. But the seventh day you shall march around the city seven times, and the priests shall blow the trumpets. It shall come to pass, when they make a long *blast* with the ram's horn, *and* when you hear the sound of the trumpet, that all the people shall shout with a great shout; then the wall of the city will fall down flat. And the people shall go up every man straight before him."

I think that God wanted more than just to conquer Jericho. He'd arrived on the scene to conquer Israel's heart. It's very possible that He instructed Joshua to use the heavenly crossfire seen in Isaiah chapter 6, the heavenly host circling the throne of God crying, 'Holy, Holy, Holy!' The sound was so loud that it moved the doorposts in Heaven. Israel followed this same circling pattern at Jericho.

Fact or Fiction

Many skeptics have scoffed at the biblical story of Jericho, but science supports it. Reynald Francisco wrote an article on "The Fall of Jericho: From an Engineer's Perspective." In it he says the following:

> I am not trying to discredit here the miracle that was accounted in the book of Joshua. On the contrary, what I'm trying to say is that it is not impossible to happen. Many Bible critics may claim that that incident described in Joshua 6 is pure folklore, exaggerated by time as it is passed from mouth to mouth. I highly disagree on this. As an engineer, I know that what happened then is true and can be explained by science. The miracle is not that the walls of Jericho fell. The miracle is how such a people of primitive knowledge of theory on resonance and wave physics made the walls collapse. The answer of course is given by the Bible: they were instructed by God.
>
> To a careful observer, the details matter. What Joshua and the rest of the soldiers did was to march around the walls. They had a trumpet sounding in front of them so it makes sense to assume that their steps were in cadence. They did this for six days. On the seventh day, they repeated the march and went around the walls seven times. Now according to Numbers 1:46, there were 603,550 men who were fit for military service. Now imagine more than half a million men marching in cadence. The march would sure produce vibration enough to shake the ground.
>
> Now it doesn't end there. At the end of the seventh march, they all (more than half a million men) gave a loud and accordant shout. Then they finally had the trumpets blow ONE LONG NOTE. That made the walls fall. Now the question is, is that

even possible? How can a march and a shout and one long note make the strongest walls of ancient eastern world fall? The answer is physics. It is an application of the mechanics of waves and the concept of resonance. Can this happen even in the modern world?[23]

As an engineer, Reynald Francisco understood the physics that caused the wall around Jericho to fall. It's too bad that the British Army didn't have a physicist on staff in 1831. Built in 1826, the Broughton Suspension Bridge was an iron chain bridge that spanned the River Irwell in Salford, Greater Manchester, England. In 1831, a contingent of marching soldiers stepped in cadence across the bridge. They had no idea that the vibrations would bring down the bridge, with them on it. It was similar to what happened at Jericho.

Six months of hardcore focus and alignment can put
you five years ahead in life. Don't underestimate
the power of consistency and desire.
– Zig Zigler

In an article called "Can A Contingent Of Marching Soldiers Collapse A Bridge?" published in *Science ABC*, they reported, "This phenomenon is based on the simple principle of frequency, which aids and abets these destructive consequences. Frequency is the number of oscillations or vibrations that occur in a unit of time. To understand this better, imagine a pendulum swinging. The faster the pendulum swings, the greater its frequency.[24]

Praise as a Weapon

Another extraordinary miracle in the Bible related to music is found in 2 Chronicles 20. As usual, the children of Israel found themselves facing insurmountable odds. A great multitude of people, including the armies of Ammon, Moab and Mt. Seir, gathered against King Jehoshaphat.

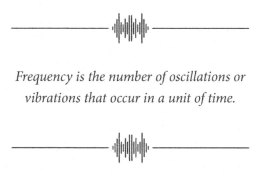

Frequency is the number of oscillations or vibrations that occur in a unit of time.

"And Jehoshaphat feared, and set himself to seek the LORD, and proclaimed a fast throughout all Judah. So Judah gathered together to ask *help* from the LORD; and from all the cities of Judah they came to seek the LORD," (2 Chronicles 20:3-4).

The king and the people of Israel were afraid and didn't know what to do. They gathered to pray and tell the Lord that their eyes were on Him. They didn't try to figure this out on their own. Rather, they waited upon the Lord. "O our God, will You not judge them? For we have no power against this great multitude that is coming against us; nor do we know what to do, but our eyes *are* upon You," (2 Chronicles 20:12).

They didn't get up and leave once they'd prayed. They stayed there, waiting on the Lord until He spoke to them through Jahaziel,

> And he said, "Listen, all you of Judah and you inhabitants of Jerusalem, and you, King Jehoshaphat! Thus says the LORD to you: 'Do not be afraid nor dismayed because of this great multitude, for the battle *is* not yours, but God's. You will not *need* to fight in this *battle*. Position yourselves, stand still

and see the salvation of the LORD, who is with you, O Judah and Jerusalem!' Do not fear or be dismayed; tomorrow go out against them, for the LORD *is* with you," (2 Chronicles 20:15,17).

God told them, "I've got this. Leave it to me." King Jehoshaphat bowed down with his face to the ground, and the people stood up to praise the Lord with a very loud voice.

The next day, they rose early. Trusting what God had said through the prophet, they made a human barrier between Jerusalem and the enemy. Then came the miracle borne on music. Jehoshaphat appointed singers who *led* the army into battle, praising God for His mercies.

They didn't go to battle singing warm, fuzzy songs celebrating I, me, and we. They ascribed all glory to *God*, and to *Him alone*. They gave the faith command for everyone to praise the Lord, holding nothing back. This aggressive, God-focused praise created an atmosphere of glory, which opened a way for miracles.

There is a reality that many self-determined, sophisticated thinkers don't want to admit. Most conflicts have a definitive spiritual component: the battle between darkness and light, right and wrong, God and Satan.

Judah had been chosen by God to produce the Messiah. Satan orchestrated this group of nations to destroy Judah in order to prevent the coming of the Messiah. However, Jehoshaphat's aggressive prayer and praise assault was much more effective than combat weapons.

Underneath the praise was a nationwide program of fasting and prayer. This very focused assault of divine frequencies caused those armies to fall into a confused, confounded hysteria that led to uncontrollable panic.

Three armies had come together to attack Israel. Without warning, two armies turned against the third and killed them all. Then the two remaining armies turned on each other and destroyed one another. Verse 22 says that the Lord set ambushments against them. The original Hebrew text defines ambushments as lying in wait, concealed and undetectable.

I'm persuaded that there were angel armies involved. Those soldiers became confused and disoriented. They couldn't think straight. It's very possible that the divine frequencies of the Levites and their passionate loud praise rearranged the atmosphere and altered the enemies' ability to see and hear.

When Israel arrived, they saw dead bodies everywhere; none had escaped. The spoil included precious jewels, and it took them three days to gather it all. They returned to Jerusalem in total victory. No fight. Not one life lost. Tons of treasure.

The fear of God rested on the lips of everyone for miles around. The Israelites played their musical instruments, sang, shouted, and danced before God at the house of the Lord.

God used the supernatural power of music to preserve His covenant people. Determine now to worship and praise God through your difficult times. Don't praise him *for* the problems. Praise Him *through* the problems.

There's no doubt that when we trust Him and walk in faith, we'll go through difficulties and come out on the other side with peace, provision, assurance, and promotion.

Worship at Midnight

On Sunday mornings, most of us sit in our lush pews, some still holding our lattes. As praise and worship begins, we're treated to easy-to-read lyrics on jumbo screens, colored light shows and beautiful music. Most of us in the Western church would have a difficult time imagining the gravity of Paul and Silas' situation.

We've discussed earlier how they were beaten and tossed into prison for delivering a young girl from a spirit of divination. They were really imprisoned for cutting off the money source from her pimp-like handlers. They were stripped naked and dragged into the innermost part of the prison.

Having toured a few of those ancient tombs of incarceration, allow me to paint a vivid picture of their surroundings. The inner part of the prison was the darkest, most dreaded place to be. They stood in raw sewage, surrounded by rats, insects and other vermin. The smell of decaying corpses still hanging in chains triggered their gag reflexes. It was in this kind of hopeless squalor that Paul and Silas made the history changing decision to pray and sing loud praises to God.

They may have quoted the words of Tertullian to the early martyrs. "The leg feels not the stocks when the mind is in heaven. Though the body is held fast, all things lie open in the spirit."[25] It's possible that Paul and Silas were in stocks that night.

> At midnight, Paul and Silas were praying and singing hymns to God, and the prisoners were listening to them. Suddenly there was a great earthquake, so that the foundations of the prison were shaken; and immediately all the doors were opened and everyone's chains were loosed. And the keeper of the prison, awaking from sleep and seeing the prison doors open, supposing the prisoners had fled, drew his sword and was about to kill himself. But Paul called with a loud voice, saying, "Do yourself no harm, for we are all here."
>
> Then he called for a light, ran in, and fell down trembling before Paul and Silas. And he brought them out and said, "Sirs, what must I do to be saved?" So they said, "Believe on the Lord Jesus Christ, and you will be saved, you and your household (Acts 16:25-31)."

If God sent an earthquake that removed my chains and the doors of my cell flew open, I'd be tempted to run. But that's not what Paul and Silas did. Instead, they stayed in their cell and stopped the jailer from killing himself. Then they led the jailer and all of his family in the prayer of salvation and baptized them.

Many Bible scholars believe that the church in Philippi sprang from that event and was pastored by the jailer. Paul's missionary journey brought the

Gospel through Macedonia, to all of Europe, and eventually to each person reading this book today. It was a living testament to the supernatural power of music, praise and worship.

CHAPTER TWENTY

MUSIC IN THE NAZI DEATH CAMPS

Anyone interested in music's power and scope must pull back a few dusty curtains of history and take a hard look at its shadowy backdrop. Music isn't exclusive to the sanitized, predictable, sometimes myopic Western world perspective.

Music has shown up everywhere, from the dawn of time until the present, expressing, communicating, chronicling, and defining life at every level. This chapter is designed to give us a reality check. Music is used for good and for evil. Under Satan's directives, the power of music has been used to suppress and destroy life. Not just any life, but the lives of God's original elect, His Covenant First Family, the Jewish people.

We will consider the demonic, dark world that distorts music's power.

The message in John 10:10 applies to music as well as anything else. "The thief does not come except to steal, and to kill, and to destroy. I [Jesus] have come that they may have life, and that they may have it more abundantly."

Satan's goal is to steal, kill and destroy – to separate the redeemed from the benefits of their covenant with God. Since Lucifer oversaw worship in Heaven, you can be sure that he understands the power of using sound and light and, especially music, to influence and control.

Here's how this chapter happened. Late one night as I was researching and praying about the content for this book, the presence of God filled my study. I leaned back in my chair, closed my eyes and said aloud, "What is it, Lord?"

I sensed a sudden ramping up of His palpable intensity, and I understood that this was very important to Him. In my spirit, where revelation interfaces with the outside world, I heard these words in a serious, resolute tone. *"I want you to include a reference to the Nazi ghettos, concentration camps, and death camps and the role music played in the life and death of my covenant people, the Jews. This is very important to me, and I trust you."*

Then He said something that I wasn't expecting.

"Get online and look at the Nazi death camp records for your family surname, Mink."

I took a deep breath, leaned forward in my chair, and moved my fingers across the keyboard of my computer. The screen came to life, and I released gut-wrenching sobs as I read name after name – *my* name, *Mink*, on those death lists.

My Jewish roots had never been discussed in my family, but I felt a very strong mandate from the Lord to honor the reality of those events and explore data regarding music and its power to sustain or destroy.

In writing his article, "Music in Concentration Camps 1933-1945," Guido Fackler completed extensive archive work, the study of memoirs and literature, as well as interviews with witnesses. His research presents an in-depth review of how music was used in the camps. He tells it all—the good, the bad, and the ugly.

Music held a significant place for almost every camp inmate in some way. This includes Nazi camps which grew into thousands of various kinds. Despite what most people believe, music was an integral part of almost all Nazi camps.

Music on Demand

The most common type of music—and torture—was singing on command. Anytime and anyplace, inmates were ordered to strike up a song. The guards used this to frighten, humiliate, and degrade them.

Eberhard Schmidt from Sachsenhausen concentration camp said, "Anyone who did not know the song was beaten. Anyone who sang too softly was beaten. Anyone who sang too loud was beaten. The SS lashed out wildly."[26]

Music was often used as punishment. For instance, Joseph Drexel in Mauthausen concentration camp was forced to sing "Jesus' Blood and Wounds" while being flogged to the point of unconsciousness.

Prisoners were often ordered to sing songs with obscene words which produced a deep sense of shame. Different camps had their own songs, most being anti-Semitic. The camp song for Buchenwald was called "Jews Song." The lyrics said, "For hundreds of years we cheated the people/ no swindle was too outrageous/ we wangled, we lied, we cheated, we narked/ whatever the currency, the crown or the mark."[27] They were forced to sing cruel, slanderous lies about themselves, their ancestors and their neighbors.

The world is a dangerous place to live; not because
of the people who are evil, but because of the people
who won't do anything about it.
– Albert Einstein

Another way they used music to demoralize prisoners was to play it continuously over loud speakers. They used national music and propaganda at Dachau to "re-educate" inmates.

Another feature of command music was the existence of camp orchestras. The musicians played as directed by the SS. The camp commander at Esterwegen concentration camp was a music lover. In addition to the camp orchestra, he had a camp choir.

"Will Stein directed this sixteen-member musical group, which rehearsed in hut number 12. The music was in the tradition of a medium-sized drawing room orchestra, playing popular classics and a higher form of light music known as *salonmusik*. Among the main tasks of the ensemble was to perform concerts in the camp square for fellow prisoners, although guards were also part of the audience. However, while the apparent or ostensible purpose of these concerts was to entertain and edify the prisoners, they were, in fact, designed for a different purpose. When a delegation from the International Red Cross visited the camp in October 1935, the commander used the ensemble for propaganda: musical performances were used to make things seem better than they were; and the world was deceived as to the real purpose of the camps."[28]

Camp commanders considered it prestigious to have a prisoners' orchestra. Ambitious men used them to improve their status within the Nazi regime.

The most gruesome role of the camp orchestra was to play for punishment and executions. On July 30, 1942, Hans Bonarewitz tried to escape from Mauthausen. He was caught and led to his execution by the camp ensemble, past all the other inmates standing in ranks.

Ericka Rothschild remembered that "the prisoners were driven out of the cattle trucks and lined up. During this process, a band made up of the best musicians from among the prisoners, were forced to march into camp as the rest were driven into the crematorium."[29]

Some musicians were forced to provide light music for the Nazis' drinking sessions, orgies and feasts.

Music Initiated by Prisoners

Prisoners also used their own initiative to perform. Sometimes it triggered memories so painful that they fell deeper into depression. However, many times music provided them with emotional support and consolation. It helped them express their feelings regarding their circumstances and living under the very real threat of imminent death.

That comfort wasn't limited to just playing instruments. Fackler found in his research that singing, humming, and whistling helped them to relax and survive the hopelessness that often drove them to suicide.

The period between 1942 and 1943 became the most prolific for forming musical groups. It became easier to obtain instruments and sheet music, as well as to form groups and give concerts. For instance, during that time Buchenwald offered a Jazz Big Band. Sachsenhausen offered a mouth-organ group. Falkensee had a gypsy orchestra.

Dachau had a varied musical life. For instance, Herbert Zipper was a conductor, a composer, and music teacher.

"As early as 1938 he formed an orchestra which secretly gave concerts for fellow prisoners. In February 1941 the SS gave permission for a twenty-eight member prisoners' orchestra; in 1942 there was a fifty-man orchestra performing a program of classical music, as well as a special Polish orchestra; in addition there was a string quartet, a chamber music ensemble, a Czech light orchestra, together with various soloists, choirs, and vocal groups. Furthermore, a theater group formed in 1943 was accompanied by music. In most camps, professional musicians or talented amateurs established musical groups. Some of these lasted only for a short time; others lasted longer; while others performed concerts where the artistic standard was very high. Music composed in the camp itself was also performed. Among the factors often preventing rehearsals and performances were the poor physical condition of the prisoners, language barriers among prisoners, the danger of being discovered, personnel changes due to deportations, the lack of instruments and sheet music; it was often necessary to organize these secretly, or to play from memory. These difficulties made it more important for professional and amateur musicians to set an example of solidarity and humane behavior in their dehumanized surroundings. This meant, of course, that there was less emphasis on aesthetic criteria: through fostering a sense of community, music served instead to form a cultural resistance, as practical assistance in the struggle to survive."[30]

Many people believe that the prisoners were never allowed to play music for themselves in the camps. That's not true. They were often allowed to play music, but any forbidden music, as that with political content, was not allowed. For instance, once when a group of prisoners played Mozart, their comrades were being flogged for the crime of Jews playing German music.

At Birkenau prisoners being marched to the gas chambers spontaneously sang the Czech national anthem or the Jewish song "Hatikvah." This was how they protested, showing that they may have been tortured and murdered, but they hadn't been broken.

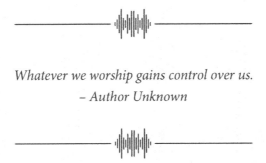

Whatever we worship gains control over us.
– Author Unknown

At night, after the SS men had left the camp, the prisoners performed block performances. These included such things as short talks, performances and songs. They were performed for improvised celebrations of a birthday, when a prisoner was released, or for any reason of personal significance.

At Dachau, Christian clergy kept up musical activities once the camp commander granted permission in the early 1940s to hold mass or other religious services.

Several camps held Christmas parties and variety shows. All inmates could attend. Although subject to censorship, these usually took place with the permission of the SS.

During Christmas and New Year 1943 and 1944, an opera was performed called "The Denizens of Buchenwald House." The opera told the story of the prisoner's ongoing battle with lice. All the prisoners knew that the lice symbolized the SS.

Never Forgotten

In addition to Mr. Fackler's article, I suggest further personal study about the music of the Holocaust. The internet has hundreds of resources available. In addition, you might consider the book *The Dairy of a Young Girl: Anne Frank* by B.M. Mooyaart. I also recommend the following films:

1959, 1967, 1980—The Dairy of Anne Frank

1982—Sophie's Choice

1980—The Pianist

1993—Schindler's List

2008—The Boy in the Striped Pajamas

You can also hear *Hatikvah*, the song sung as Jewish prisoners filed into the extermination chambers. This song is now the Israeli national anthem.

Some New World Order historians, used as pawns of Satan, are desperate to have us rewrite history and erase the Holocaust. They would like nothing more than to erase from memory over ten million people they consider undesirable. They would have us forget their lives, destinies, talents, fortunes, and influence on the world.

Divine edict demands that we not only remember this unthinkable crime against humanity, but that we celebrate those who suffered there. This kind of mass racial extermination has happened all over the world for thousands of years, yet music survives and thrives through it all.

Auschwitz survivor Shoshana Kalisch testifies:

Yes, we sang in the ghettos and concentration camps. Songs were sung even in the death camps. They were the only means of expressing our sadness and grief, defiance and hope. When our spirits sank, the songs took over; they helped us to keep our faith that life held some meaning. The only possible form of resistance was spiritual.[31]

Though dehumanized by the Nazi regime, through singing, death camp captives could distinguish themselves from the animals that others believed them to be.

Throughout history unspeakable tragedies – slavery, ethnic cleansing, wars, and natural disasters – have shown us many things. We've learned that whether used for worship, resistance, chronicling history, survival, or social commentary, music has always been an affirmation of life, showing that even though circumstances are horrific, the human spirit will continue to sing.

Before we leave the holocaust behind, I think we should take this time to consider Isaiah 61:1-7 from *The Voice* translation. I believe this passage in this translation speaks a clear message to both the victims and the survivors of this terrible crime.

The Spirit of the Lord, the Eternal, is on me.

The Lord has appointed me for a special purpose.

He has anointed me to bring good news to the poor.

He has sent me to repair broken hearts,

And to declare to those who are held captive and bound in prison,

"Be free *from your imprisonment!*"

He has sent me to announce the year *of jubilee, the season* of the Eternal's favor:

for our enemies it will be a day of God's wrath;

For those who mourn it will be *a time of* comfort.

As for those who grieve over Zion,

God has sent me to give them a *beautiful* crown in exchange for ashes,

To anoint them with gladness instead of sorrow,

to wrap them in *victory, joy, and* praise instead of depression and sadness.

People will call them *magnificent, like great towering* trees

standing for what is right.

They stand to the glory of the Eternal who planted them.

And they will rebuild *this place from* its ancient ruins;

they will restore the ages-old, *once-splendid* structures;

They will renew *Israel's* ruined cities

from the ashes and debris that lay *untouched* for

many generations.

And people will come from all over *to serve you*:

Outsiders will tend your flocks, plough your fields, and prune your vines.

You will be known as *the ones specially* chosen by the Eternal as priests;

people will speak of you as ministers of our God.

And the wealth of nations will come to you for your delight and enrichment.

Many called you disgraced *and defiled* and said that shame should be your share of things.

Yet you suffered doubly and lived in disgrace;

So double will be your share, and with joy everlasting.

CHAPTER TWENTY-ONE

THE BENEFITS OF MUSIC

Music has a strong influence, and it has the power to persuade. It affects retail sales, restaurant ambiance, the general mood in public areas, the transportation industry, the entertainment world, and almost anything it touches. Revved up music with a driving beat in a teen clothing store promotes purchases. The right music in grocery stores triggers impulse buying.

The psychology of music in the marketplace is very complex. Each outlet can fine tune music's persuasive effect on customers and employees. Tempo, key, genre, instrumentation, and rhythmic coloration are just a few of the things which play into creating the perfect atmosphere for shoppers. Get the right music and enjoy a more profitable bottom line.

Researchers at the National Central University of Taiwan suggest that songs with 125 to 130 beats per minutes improve decision-making skills. Loud music, however, is distracting. They suggest sticking to levels no louder than your speaking voice.

Our moms were onto something when they sang us to sleep with lullabies. Rick Notter, author of *Sound Advice: Music's Effect on Life, Health, and Happiness* says, "Music is good for calming the nervous system. Soft, slow-tempo music is good to play in the background when discussing finances or reviewing your budget."

Behavioral psychologist Matt Wallert says, "The middle of the musical road is the best balancing place." He explains that songs that are around 100 beats per minute will keep your blood pressure from hitting the roof while keeping your mood elevated and upbeat.

This makes an even stronger case for creating your own playlists and using them in the car, while exercising, praying, or worshiping. You can provide each area of your life with its own musical frequencies to optimize your experience.

Beware of social media's propensity for raising anxiety levels by overloading your brain with senseless data that can get you off track. Finding out that your former boyfriend is married is a good example. Being informed is fine; worrying about why you're still single is not.

Ethnic music enhances the atmosphere at restaurants, drawing the guest into the experience. With each person's search for significance, the server's suggestion to try a new item on the menu is met with less resistance. It may have been a delightful experience, but the music assisted in your paying a higher price for dinner. Higher prices equal higher tips.

Subliminal messages are high-speed, high-frequency messages, undetectable to the human ear but received by the human brain. These hidden messages, buried within music, can implant information deep into our subconscious minds. Then they telegraph their content to the conscious mind and influence choices and outward behavior.

Within perception lies the foundation for decision making. This reality can manifest in both positive and negative choices. It depends a great deal on the content of the message received and the strength of the hearer's belief system.

Subliminal messaging can show up not only within music, but also in visual arts and advertising. At one time, movie theaters flashed a 1/3000th second picture of soda and popcorn every few seconds throughout a film. These were too fast for the eye to see, but not too fast for the brain to process. Sales of popcorn soared.

Churches whose music is dark, ultra-reflective, slow in tempo with instruments voiced in minor keys, often experience an eventual downturn in giving. This holds especially true if the lyrics lead participants to see themselves as lowly worms, victims of life's battles and losing all the time.

If you attend a church like that, I have a very short, one-word piece of advice: *RUN.*

Music's Social Influence

Regardless of musical differences, upbringing, exposure, or world view, I've seldom heard anyone say, "I hate every kind of music!" However, we've all heard of music being blamed for polluting young minds or leading millions over a moral precipice.

While music may give a teenager an outlet from dysfunctional families, it's also possible for it to undergird and affirm anti-social behaviors. Lest we begin a witch hunt driven by self-righteousness, let's investigate the real culprits behind rebellion, crime, violence, and other social toxins.

Most negative behavior emerges from families that are in trouble. Physical and emotional abuse often are the destructive forces at work in these homes. There are many fatherless homes today where fear and insecurity thrive. There is also the crippling reality of poverty and its resulting fruit.

Critics often blame music for these problems. The people who write it say, "We're just telling it like it is; music mirrors the realities of society."

The truth lies somewhere in the middle of these two perspectives. Reporting and recording the problem is not being part of the answer. Nor is always sounding the alarm while offering no life changing alternatives.

While musical styles and genres come and go, they will always be dragged into the discussion of society's woes. While it's true that music needs to be created and performed with responsibility, it never commits crimes—people do.

Music will forever be the art form that best expresses feelings of the heart. That goes all the way from the highest praise of God down to the most vulgar of animal instincts. The bedrock is that people need to change, and music can help make that happen.

When young people attempt to claim a unique identity, they often fail to see that those rugged individuals all end up looking and sounding the same. Instead of being unique, they end up being cookie cutter replicas. In their search for significance, they're easy prey for music, films, social media and clothing designers who advertise the coolest look, sound, or behavior. These are greed-driven industries in which the teenagers are merely pawns.

Most kids make it through that media-bombarded, hormone-soaked minefield. Increasing numbers, however, act out with unspeakable violence against society. The rest of us look for someone to blame: wimpy fathers, the watered-down message of the church, the educational system, politicians, music, and videos games. The list goes on *ad nauseum.*

The truth is that these things are symptoms of the real problem. We've drifted away from a relationship with God. The root of all our problems revolves around *character.* Only intimacy with God, however it must come, can start the slow process of turning the ship of our society in the right direction. Music plays a pivotal role in turning our hearts towards home.

Music and Patriotism

Nothing stirs the heart quite like a musical piece that evokes emotion and moves a group of people toward a common goal. From the beginning of recorded history, almost every culture has embraced some form of a musical rallying point. It might be an allegiance to a country. Our hearts swell with pride, and lumps form in our throats, when we sing our national anthem.

Each culture has a musical arsenal that forges unity with every beat. In biblical times, they used rams' horns, called *shofars,* and brass trumpets to give instructions *en masse.* Today, our military has an enduring example of this from reveille to taps and everything in between.

Music stirs patriotism and *esprit de corps,* moving us to unified purpose and spurring superhuman acts of selfless heroism. You may have seen the war movie, *Bridge on the River Kwai.* I can still hear "Colonel Bogey March," the unforgettable song the soldiers whistled together in triumph in the face of barbaric treatment by the enemy. Many marching bands, drum and bugle corps, and mass singing groups were designed to uplift and unite.

Military music has often been used to demoralize the enemy, as well. One such example happened when bagpipes played in combat situations. There is something supernatural and spiritual about bagpipes. If you ever saw the movie *The Longest Day*, I doubt you could forget the scene when the bagpipes played "Black Bear" and lifted our spirits,

Some of the most common bagpipe tunes played throughout history were "Scotland the Brave," "Wings," "Battle of Waterloo" and everyone's favorite, "Amazing Grace." I'll admit that I still cry whenever I hear bagpipes play.

During the war, those playing the bagpipes were targeted and gunned down so often that after World War I, they were ordered to play only in the trenches so that the soldiers could hear the music for as long as possible.

Another example of percussive and vocal music being used as instruments of war is found among the Zulu people. During tribal conflicts and foreign invasions, Zulu warriors ran for miles in cadence. They chanted and struck their wood and cowhide shields with their spears in rhythm with their cadence. Their enemies heard and felt it from miles away. It struck such fear in their hearts that sometimes they ran away before the Zulus arrived.

The military has used music to train and teach soldiers for years. The instructor sings out a line, and then the troops sing the same line in reply. This makes physical training so much more effective as musical cadence multiplies strength. Applying music in military settings develops unity among the troops and improves corporate force.

During traumatic events, songs help people survive. Those songs often chronicle victory or defeat, keeping history alive for posterity.

Of course, we can't forget the songs written from the heart about that special someone. Romantic songs can evoke feelings, and even smells, from deep in memory. Music brings events and emotions stored in our memory into the present. That's why we often hear someone say,

"They're playing our song."

Music records the past, penetrates all barriers, transcends time, teaches, and rehearses life lessons. It deals with the realities of the present and sets blueprints in place for dreams of the future.

Music sets mileposts in our lives.

Laughter Really is the Best Medicine

No book on music would be complete without mentioning the deep therapeutic power of music. So many experiences revolve around music as it pertains to humor, laughing, singing funny songs, and enjoying the closeness of human bonding. It seems to add layers of effectiveness to a joke or funny story. Rhyme and melody can make humorous situations even funnier. Recalling funny songs, situations, or jokes is vital because we all want to spread joy. But it isn't just for fun.

There are many levels of happiness and joy. Happiness is often present when everything is going well. However, joy is not dependent on circumstances. Joy comes from a relationship with God. The joy of the Lord is not the joy God gives us to fill up our joy reservoir. It's not like stopping by a gas station when the car is on empty.

The joy of the Lord grows from our being permanently attached to His supply of joy. You'll never run out because He never runs out. That's why we can experience supernatural joy even during the worst circumstances.

Any preacher, corporate leader, or teacher worth his salt becomes skillful at using real, family-style humor. I've heard it said that, "A comedian tells funny stories, but a humorist tells stories funny." A musician, though, can make a funny story unforgettable.

Humor also breaks the ice in communication. My father, Myers Mink, was born in 1917 and raised in Bulls Gap, Tennessee. During the Great Depression, my grandparents, who had seven or eight children, ran a boarding house. Usually young, single men rented rooms and ate two meals a day there. One of those young men was Archie Campbell, later of *Grand Ole Opry* and *Hee Haw* fame.

Dad said that Archie was a good looking young singer. Each evening, he sat on the front porch with his guitar. He sang songs, told jokes and always drew a crowd. Dad's side of the family had the same inclinations, so the songs and hilarity grew to epic proportions.

Archie went into show business with song, dance, and humor. Dad went other directions in his life, but always saw to it that corny, hilarious jokes were inserted into our lives at appropriate moments. (The apple didn't fall far from the tree in my case.)

My direction went toward music. You can praise God that you won't have to hear all of my corny, sometimes hilarious jokes.

I'm including a short article called "Do Not Wipe That Smile Off Your Face," written by Kenneth Cole:

> Laughter is an important part of a healthy life. Like a nutritious diet and exercise, positive emotions are necessary to keep us on an even keel, physically and psychologically. Laughter helps reduce anxiety and tension in school, at work or at play, with relationships and just everyday living.
>
> It is one of the most important characteristics we can give children. It profoundly affects their coping abilities and relationships with the world around them. Parents can start to teach their children about the health benefits of laughter with a few facts:
>
> When people laugh or cry hard, their heart rate quickens, their lungs expand and fill to capacity, their throat goes into uncoordinated spasms, all capillaries open, and the pituitary gland is stimulated to produce natural painkillers a hundred times more powerful than morphine. The effect is like taking the body on an internal jog.

In an era where we are taught that we can be a Christian and still pursue a life serving ourselves, we ultimately come fact-to-face with a harsh reality. Self-focus is a form of cannibalism. Feed on self, and we get sick. Feed on God and serving others, and we stay healthy. Self-possession makes us insecure and judgmental, leaving us no room in our hearts to love people.
– Len Mink

Start Your Day with Laughter

Other health care professionals extol the curative powers of laughter. Annette Goodheart, PhD., recommends faking it to feel better. Go some-place private, she advises, and start pumping out those familiar sounds – "Ha, Ha, Ha!" Oxygen floods the blood, and the cardiovascular system dilates (which is why the face gets flushed). The muscles relax (which is why you fall out of your chair if you laugh hard enough), the diaphragm con-vulses (which is why you get a pain in your side) according to Goodheart, and "the internal organs get massaged."

If you start every morning with 15 minutes of laughter, it will take care of the rest of your day. Start with 15 seconds and work up to what you can tolerate. Try it. It works.

Alison Crane, R.N., notes that a good laugh changes blood pressure (blood pressure rises during laughter, but lowers to below the starting point afterward), reduces muscle tension, improves digestion and, if you laugh enough to cry, tears will be released that contain bacteria-killing agents.

Laughter can also improve communication between people. Shared laughter can create community and facilitate the sense of belonging. Fear, loneliness, and isolation disappear in shared laughter. Laughter and play is a total philosophy, not just a good-time philosophy.

Annette Godheart, Ph.D., says, "Laughter is an untapped science and a treasure chest of benefits always available to us."

A good sense of humor is a vital key to a successful marriage, business venture or any activity worth pursuing. After all, Psalm 2:4 says, "He who sits in the heavens laughs; the Lord holds them [his enemies] in derision," (ESV).

Proverb 17:22 says, "A merry heart does good like a medicine, but a broken spirit dries the bones."

The Joy of the Lord is Your Strength

While laughter makes the heart merry, the joy of the Lord is our strength. In life, we encounter a stream of challenges which can turn into negative feelings. We're grateful for the many victories that punctuate our journey, but too many challenges may suppress the joy factor in our lives. Staying full of God's Word to the point of overflow is a key element of developing a life filled with joy, always facing life from a position of strength,

We learn in Nehemiah 8:10 that the joy of the Lord is our strength. And Nehemiah continued, "Go and celebrate with a feast of rich foods and sweet drinks, and share gifts of food with people who have nothing prepared. This is a sacred day before our Lord. Don't be dejected and sad, for the joy of the LORD is your strength!" (NLT).

If we're the reservoir of joy for our own lives, our capacity is always limited. But if we've tapped into God's unending supply, there's abundance no matter what you're going through. God's joy for us is so great that He came to earth as Jesus to purchase our salvation.

The reality is: *His* joy is in *you*.

Hebrews 12:2 says, "looking unto Jesus, the author and finisher of *our* faith, who for the joy that was set before Him endured the cross, despising the shame, and has sat down at the right hand of the throne of God."

As much as God loves giving us joy, we also give Him joy. Consider the pearl of great price: "Again, the kingdom of heaven is like a merchant seeking beautiful pearls, who, when he had found one pearl of great price, went and sold all that he had and bought it," (Matt. 13:45-46).

Many people teach that Jesus is that pearl of great price. In the context of Hebrews 12:2, it seems that *we* are the pearl that He purchased with His life so that we could be with Him forever.

Why would He want that? Because we give Him joy.

Isaiah 65:19 says, "I will rejoice in Jerusalem, And joy in My people..."

Zephaniah 3:17 says, "The LORD your God is in your midst, a mighty one who will save; he will rejoice over you with gladness; he will quiet you by his love; he will exult over you with loud singing." Music seems to be the Divine choice for God to express His joy toward us.

Hebrews 1:9 says, "You have loved righteousness and hated wickedness; therefore God, your God, has anointed you with the oil of gladness beyond your companions."

His joy is the fruit of His passion for what is right and His hatred for what is wicked. This is important to Him because He knows the effects of both forces on His beloved—*You.*

John 15:10 tells us, "If you keep My commandments, you will abide in My love, just as I have kept My Father's commandments and abide in His love."

God's heart of love towards us rejoices when we allow His joy to make *our* joy full. His joy is our strength.

Music, praise, worship, and songs have the power to invade and quicken every quantum particle of our beings. They infuse us with vast supplies of God's joy into every crack and crevice, conscious and subconscious. That's why so many issues entrenched deep into our human psyche can be accessed and neutralized through the power of song.

We've never seen the glorious face of our Savior. Our love and devotion to Jesus is 100 percent by faith. It comes with purity of motive and a love for Jesus that invokes glory into the atmosphere. It allows God to manifest Himself in every area of our lives.

Worship, based on the Word of God, is the express lane that takes you to miracles, joy, purpose, identity, and power.

Music and the World of Children

A school in Bynum, Montana, has gone back to traditional music education in early elementary grades. Every morning, all the students dance and sing for 20 minutes before beginning their academic work. They use folk dances so that each person has a partner, changing until every child has danced with each other.

They've found that this promotes unity and releases the positive aspects of singing and responding to music in a physical way. This traditional music education teaches history, as well as promoting a sense of stability within the school population. It also provides more stability outside the school in the community and in the students' homes. It offers benefits that are physical, mental, and depending on the music chosen, spiritual.

They also sing the National Anthem each morning, in three or four vocal parts, which enhances their sense of patriotism and national pride.[32]

I was blessed to grow up in a time and place where we did these same things every day. What a wonderful experience. It grounded us and taught us a great deal about life, respect for others, and love for God. I encourage parents to do these same fun things as extracurricular activities with your youngsters. They'll be richer and smarter for it. Break the media addictions; give the videos games and cell phones a rest.

There are a tremendous number of benefits to children who have music integrated into their early lives. Early literacy is formed by building sound/word recognition and visual word recognition and comprehension. These are building blocks for reading.

Music develops creative freedom and inspires children to explore many possibilities of expression. Physical development and coordination are enhanced by moving, dancing, and acting out the sounds and emotions they create. It also fine tunes large and small motor skills.

Music helps children listen, interact, and respond to others. This occurs both in a group settings and one-on-one, creating good manners and interaction boundaries. Music helps the brain to develop spatial-temporal and reasoning skills required for math, science, and engineering.

Linking familiar melodies to new information can imprint the child with knowledge about important subjects. Music education creates vast improvements in creative thinking and problem solving. It also increases grades in high school and improves overall SAT scores.

Music education has been shown to help decentralize the controlling attitude of the "Me First" mindset that's so prevalent today. Cooperating with others to reach a common goal raises respect levels toward others – especially toward children from other cultures or with special needs. In other words, we can teach and admonish through song.

The Bible says, "Let the word of Christ dwell in you richly in all wisdom, teaching and admonishing one another in psalms and hymns and spiritual songs, singing with grace in your hearts to the Lord," (Colossians 3:16).

Music performance teaches young people to step up to the plate, conquer fear, and take risks. They learn that a little anxiety while pursuing excellence is a part of life. Dealing with this early helps them later in life. Those who don't learn to deal with stress and anxiety early often turn to drugs or other risky behaviors in an effort to cope.

Music, though flexible and infinitely variable, is composed of absolutes. A mistake is a mistake. Voices and other instruments are either in tune or not. Meter is an absolute. Children learn the value of sustained effort through practice. They also experience the rewards that excellence offers. Music creates balance and boundaries in their lives.

Children and music go together like cookies and milk.

Physical Benefits of Music

There are numerous positive effects that music provides on the entire body. Here are a few:

Pain Relief. Studies have shown that music demonstrates positive effects by reducing the intensity of pain in geriatric care, intensive care and palliative care.

Improves Sleep. Listening to classical music has been shown to treat insomnia in college students.

Eat Less. One study found that playing music during a meal can help people relax, slow down and eat less.

Improves Blood Vessel Function. Scientists have discovered that the emotions patients experience while listening to music have positive effects on how their blood vessels function. Music makes them feel happier and results in increased blood flow in their blood vessels.

Reduces Stress. Research has found that listening to music relieves stress by triggering biochemical stress reducers.

Induces a Meditative State. Listening to slow musical beats alters brain wave speed, creating brain wave activity similar to when a person is meditating. It can also ease symptoms of migraines and PMS and improve behavioral issues.

Relieves Symptoms of Depression. Classic [sic] and meditative music are uplifting and improve symptoms of depression.

Heavy metal and techno music have been shown to make symptoms of depression worse.

Elevates Mood. A 2013 study found that music put people in better moods and helped them get into touch with their feelings.

Improves Cognitive Function. Listening to background music improves your brain power. It allowed test takers to answer more questions in the allotted time and get more answers right. Some studies indicate that music improves cognitive skills best if it first improves a person's emotional state.

Improves Performance in High Pressure Situations. Studies show that basketball players who perform poorly under pressure, experienced significant improvement during high pressure free-throw shooting if they first listened to upbeat music and lyrics.

Improves Recovery in Stroke Patients. Researchers in Finland found that stroke patients experienced verbal memory improvement when they listened to music for two hours a day.[33]

Research plus good old fashioned life experience keeps revealing more and more benefits from a life infused with musical revelations. The gift of music just keeps on giving!

CHAPTER TWENTY-TWO

MUSIC AND BRAIN FUNCTION

Did you ever consider that music might make you smarter? Numerous studies of the effects of music on the brain suggest that it does. For instance, one study revealed that classical music from Christian masters is not only soothing—it makes you smarter.

If you took piano lessons for a while as a child but didn't stick with it, there is good news for you. Having some type of musical background has measurable effects on the brain. This is great news for parents who spent time and money providing music lessons for unmotivated children.

In a study performed at the University of Daytona, 56 subjects were examined for cognitive function after listening to music. They listened to 10 partial pieces of Mozart's fast-tempo works. Each time, the rate of brain processing increased, as did linguistic processing accuracy. A recent article published in PubMed found that this increased cognition was especially true in older adults.

It appears that God's gift of music has a major impact on us. Rather than spending hours listening to the news, current events, and entertainment, we can listen to music and get smarter.

One of the many known things that music does is improve the blood flow to the cerebrum. It also enhances the release and transport of dopamine, which makes everyone feel better. Listening to music improves both memory and learning.

There is an abundance of research on brain function, so it isn't surprising that people often use music at work to support their thinking. Some studies suggest that music affects the brain via an improvement in the emotions.

In one study, 54 participants with no musical training, looked at a collection of 300 faces. One group looked at the faces while listening to emotionally touching or joy-filled music. The other group had no music. Those who heard music remembered many more faces than those who did not. This demonstrated a significant improvement in memory.[34]

Music can help people learn a new language or rewire the speech center in the brain after a stroke. On February 21, 2010, Victoria Gill, a science reporter for BBC News in San Diego, published this article, "Singing 'rewires' damaged brain."

> By singing, patients use a different area of the brain from the area involved in speech.
>
> If a person's "speech centre" is damaged by a stroke, they can learn to use their "singing centre" instead.

Researchers presented these findings at the annual meeting of the American Association for the Advancement of Science (AAAS) in San Diego.

An ongoing clinical trial, they said, has shown how the brain responds to this "melodic intonation therapy".

Gottfried Schlaug, a neurology professor at Beth Israel Deaconess Medical Center and Harvard Medical School in Boston led the trial.

The therapy is already established as a medical technique. Researchers first used it when it was discovered that stroke patients with brain damage that left them unable to speak were still able to sing.

Making connections

Most of the connections between brain areas that control movement and those that control hearing are on the left side of the brain.

"If you damage the left side, the right side has trouble [fulfilling that role]."

But as patients learn to put their words to melodies, the crucial connections form on the right side of their brains.

Previous brain imaging studies have shown that this "singing centre" is overdeveloped in the brains of professional singers.

During the therapy sessions, patients are taught to put their words to simple melodies.

Professor Schlaug said that after a single session, a stroke patient who was not able to form any intelligible words learned to say the phrase "I am thirsty" by combining each syllable with the note of a melody.

The patients are also encouraged to tap out each syllable with their hands. Professor Schlaug said that this seemed to act as an "internal pace-maker" which made the therapy even more effective.

"Music might be an alternative medium to engage parts of the brain that are otherwise not engaged," he said.

Brain sounds

Dr. Aniruddh Patel from the Neurosciences Institute in San Diego, said the study was an example of the "explosion in research into music and the brain" over the last decade.

"People sometimes ask where in the brain music is processed and the answer is everywhere above the neck," said Dr. Patel.

"Music engages huge swathes of the brain -- it's not just lighting up a spot in the auditory cortex."

Dr. Nina Kraus, a neuroscientist from Northwestern University in Chicago, also studies the effects of music on the brain.

In her research she records the brain's response to music, using electrodes on the scalp.

This work has enabled her to "play back" electrical activity from brain cells as they pick up sounds.

"Neurons work with electricity - so if you record the electricity from the brain you can play that back through speakers and hear how the brain deals with sounds," she explained.

Dr. Kraus has also discovered that musical training seems to enhance the ability to perform other tasks, such as reading. She said that the insights into how the brain responds to music provided evidence that musical training was an important part of children's education.[35]

Music is the greatest communication in the world.
Even if people don't understand the language that you're
singing in, they still know good music when they hear it.
– Lou Rawls

Parkinson's Disease

Music has the power to reestablish neuro-pathways in human memory. No one knows for certain if it is only for the duration of the musical encounter, but it shows much promise as research into Parkinson's disease and other brain disorders progresses. Parkinson's Disease is associated with degeneration of the basal ganglia of the brain. This involves voluntary motor movements, learning habits, eye movements, cognition, and emotion. Parkinson's is also a result of a deficiency of the neurotransmitter dopamine, which is vital to conduction of our neuro impulses.

Please take a moment and watch a video showing the dramatic impact music had on a patient with Parkinson's Disease. On YouTube, search for "Gait Training for Parkinson's Patient Using Music." Watch as Anicea Gunlock works with the patient without music, and see the incredible difference it makes when she plays music. The gentleman who could hardly move with his walker began to straighten up and then continued without the walker. The music had such an amazing effect that he began to dance with Anicea. This video is a must-see!

Music and Alzheimer's

There have been tremendous results in treating people with Alzheimer's Disease with music therapy. The following are excerpts from an article written by Sally Abrahms called "Tune In To Music Therapy's Healing Powers." It was published in the AARP Bulletin in March of 2013.

> Geriatrician Theresa Allison can't talk with her grandmother. Alzheimer's disease has left her without the ability to see, converse or recognize her granddaughter. Yet the two are able to interact. Instead of talking, they sing. "I've watched her babble nonsense, but then bounce my son on her knee as we sing a folk song she taught me as a child. For 45 seconds, life is completely normal," says Allison. "Engaging this way is profoundly meaningful."
>
> Allison, a musicologist as well as physician and assistant professor in the Division of Geriatrics at the University of California, San Francisco, sometimes sings songs with her frightened or confused patients to get them to relax during a physical exam. And she encourages generous doses of music in caregiving, whether the loved one is cognitively intact or has memory loss.

Lately, researchers have focused on how music can benefit those with Alzheimer's. Anecdotal evidence shows that music can tap memories and reduce anxiety, pain, heart rate, and blood pressure. It can help accelerate healing, boost learning, improve neurological disorders, and increase social interaction.

Sophisticated imaging techniques such as PET scans and MRIs are beginning to reveal the full picture. "Neuroscientists who have wondered how someone with a stroke or brain injury can recover speech by singing, or why a person with Parkinson's can walk or dance to music but not without it, have now acquired the technology to see, in real time, how music stimulates and activates networks in the brain," says Connie Tomaino, executive director of the Institute for Music and Neurologic Function in New York. The research is still in its infancy, she says, but it suggests that music may improve specific function such as speech and movement.

Select familiar songs

Most people remember music from childhood or when they were in their 20s.

Does Mom love opera or show tunes? What songs make her dance?

After former U.S. Rep. Gabrielle Giffords was shot in January 2011 and suffered brain damage, she was unable to speak. But her mother knew her favorite songs — "American Pie," "Brown Eyed Girl," "Over the Rainbow" — and along with Giffords' dad, husband, and music therapist, surrounded her with the music she loved.

"Gabby could sing several words in a phrase, but couldn't put a three-word sentence together on her own," says her music therapist, Maegan Morrow, of TIRR Memorial Hermann hospital in Houston. Morrow had her sing her needs, such as "I want to go to bed" or "I'm tired." Help your loved one recall words by singing part of a familiar song and having her finish the line with you, or alone.

"One of the best ways to get directions across is to sing, rather than speak, them," says Clair, who for 20 years has used music therapy for people with dementia.

"Never use loud, frenetic music," she warns. Need to coax a loved one into the shower? Put on Duke Ellington and dance together into the bathroom.

Make music together.

A pilot study by New York University Langone Medical Center's Comprehensive Center on Brain Aging found that members of the Unforgettables, a New York City chorus made up of those with early to mid-stage Alzheimer's and their caregiving spouses and children, reported more self-esteem, better moods, less depression, and a greater quality of life after 13 rehearsals and one concert.

Joe Fabiano, 65, has been bringing his wife, Anita, 65, to the two-hour weekly rehearsals since the chorus was formed two years ago. "This is something we can share," says Joe. "It makes me think of the old days, when we were happy." Says Anita, "It's good for my husband and helps me a lot. I like the camaraderie."

Not a singer? Consider rhythm. Drumming with others later in life is also a growing trend, according to Encinitas, California music therapist and author Christine Stevens, who teaches health care professionals and family caregivers about percussion. "You don't have to be musical whatsoever," says Stevens. In her hospital room, former Rep. Giffords participated in a drum circle with her family and friends. Remo, a drum manufacturer, offers a "health rhythms" section on their website that discusses the health benefits of drumming and how to find a drumming group.

Music can be a great source of relief and pleasure. When her husband is at adult day care, during other times of the day, or before bed, Susan Trifone will turn on the tunes. "My body gets in rhythm to the beat and it makes me feel much better. But even more, music helps me get away from my everyday problems."[36]

Praise and Mental Illness

Our society suffers from deep political division, terrorism, school shootings, an opioid crisis and spiraling mental illness. In fact, many people blame what's happening in our society on the increasing numbers of mentally ill.

The mentally ill in America have been thrown into a confusing and contradictory system of doctors, clinics, institutions, home care, and drug regimens. And yet, they are getting no better. Many people believe that we have a broken mental health system.

According to the US Department of Health and Human Services, one in five Americans has experienced issues with mental health. One in 10 youth has suffered a major bout of depression. People with severe mental illness, such as schizophrenia, bipolar disorder, or a major depressive disorder live much shorter lifespans.[37]

In the past couple of decades, mental health has become a topic of massive interest in society. This is due in large part to the overwhelming need to address pressing issues that have refused to be suppressed any longer.

Music can take us back to a time or place in our lives,
whether good or bad. It can reconnect us with a person,
location or event. It can even activate the sense of smell
stored in our memory from a certain time and place.
– Len Mink

Mass media has seen to it that we have a nonstop stream of information, twenty-four hours a day and seven days a week. Most of the information we hear is negative. Not only does the content focus on dark, toxic material, it's presented in such a way as to garner all the shock value possible.

There's an old newspaper adage: Bad news sells more papers. This mindset has evolved through a tsunami of verbal and visual pollutants. Of course, they add the occasional silver lining for the sake of respectability.

We've all heard the phrase, "You are what you eat." If that's true in nutrition, it's even more true in mental health. The Bible says it this way: "For as he thinks in his heart, so *is* he," (Proverbs 23;7a).

The human mind is like a modern computer. It can process and manage only a certain amount of input, either positive or negative. If we receive a steady diet of negative, fear-charged words and images each day, the cumulative effect on our mental state is very detrimental.

Praise Reduces Stress

It's widely known in the scientific and medical communities that the clear majority of chronic and acute diseases are related to stress. This stress is related to the information people hear daily. Over time, this will form their philosophy and interpretation of life. Their personal world view is on a steady decline. Anxiety and fear replace peace, purpose, and a sense of well being.

Praise is a tremendous adjunct to good mental health. It decentralizes our attention on ourselves and focuses our attention on God and our role in helping others find their destinies. The self-absorbed ego-driven life engages in a kind of cannibalism, feeding on itself and causing a plethora of illnesses.

It would be like a person having a plastic dome over his head and never hearing any sounds but the deafening reverberations of his own voice. However, nourishing ourselves on the plans, purposes and pursuits of God will increase divine order in our lives. It produces wholeness in every part of our lives, especially in mental health.

I believe that a full-scale emphasis on developing a personal and corporate life of praise and worship would empty many mental institutions. It would put most psychiatrists out of business. It seems apparent that all of our mental and emotional woes distill down to one basic component: Over-occupation with the personal ego, which is self-centeredness.

We must keep in mind what the Bible says about keeping our minds in peace.

"You will keep him in perfect peace, whose mind is stayed on You, because he trusts in You," (Isaiah 26:3).

Words form images that become our navigating points through life. Good images mean a higher quality of life in every area. Bad images mean a lower quality of life in every area.

History supports the fact that each time a generational curse was stopped in its tracks, it happened because someone replaced the negative images on the inside with life-filled, positive, and uplifting mind and heart pictures.

We're designed by God to produce, create, build, serve, heal, celebrate, and enjoy each season of our lives. Decisions and actions based on information received—whether accurate or in error—determine the course of each of our lives. Praise, based on a decision to decentralize ourselves, produces a forgetfulness of ourselves. That leads to good mental health.

Most problems have a spiritual root cause which can be traced to the basic conflict between spiritual darkness and light. We live in a faith universe, created by words and songs of faith. It requires faith to operate in this kind of world.

"Now faith is the substance of things hoped for, the evidence of things not seen," (Hebrews 11:1). This could be stated, "Faith is being fully persuaded and assured that those things that you anticipate with joyous and confident expectation are already yours in the here and now, based upon a contract or covenant you possess, being convinced beyond a doubt that the one who promised cannot lie," (Len Mink composite translation).

The universe was created by words of faith and is voice-activated to this day. Words of faith create images of faith, blueprints that cause all divine and human systems to bring to pass the perfect will of God as revealed in His Word.

A life filled with worship and praise evokes divine frequencies, thus creating perfect conductivity for the Word-based will of God to flow unhindered in your life.

Gospel Duck Invades the Psych Ward

One of my alter egos is a duck. Gospel Duck. He sings, talks, and teaches children about God. Over the years, we've received many wonderful testimonies about things that have happened to children — and adults — who listened to our various Gospel Duck recordings.

One such testimony is from a nurse in a juvenile psych ward at a large metropolitan hospital. She said that she began playing Gospel Duck CDs for the children. Sometimes they listened while in group therapy. Often, she played them for the children one-on-one in the child's hospital room. Over time, she noticed children showing signs of improvement in various areas of their daily lives.

One by one, the children exhibited clinical evidence that their symptoms had improved in significant ways. Doctors released them to go home to their families. "After a few months," she said, "we had no children left in our department."

She ended her story by saying that there had been no changes in therapy activities or medication. The only thing different was the introduction of Gospel Duck music and dialogue into their daily routines.

I believe that if praise music can empty a children's psych ward, it could do the same anywhere, even if sung by a duck!

CHAPTER TWENTY-THREE

A LIFESTYLE OF PRAISE AND WORSHIP

In the fall of 1971, soon after I surrendered my life to Jesus, I was diagnosed with a severe blood disease. I was still on television in Cincinnati, doing several shows. Cathy and I were delighted to go from place to place, sharing our testimony. When I learned about the blood disorder, I was gripped by the contrast between my "Jesus high" and the kick-in-the-gut medical report.

I prayed what most of us considered to be the humble Christian prayer. "Lord, if it be thy will, please heal me." I got worse. Doctors tested me and tried treatments as I struggled to do live TV each week. Strength and energy drained out of my body, and I didn't know how to make it stop.

At the University of Cincinnati College of Medicine's Hematology Department, four or five doctors worked on trying to find an answer as to why I suffered from this rare blood disease. At one appointment, the head of the department sat down and looked me in the eye. "Why didn't you tell us you were Jewish?"

"Jewish?" I asked. "I've never really known much about our family history on either side of my family. What are you saying?"

"This blood disease is quite rare, but it shows up every few generations in Jewish bloodlines. We tested your blood. Len, the blood never lies!"

That brilliant Jewish hematologist was speaking to me about his specialty: The blood. It never lies. But I knew that God was speaking through those words to remind me of the power of Jesus' blood. It never lies. Scripture never lies.

Those words spoke something different to me. I knew that I could move on from that old prayer asking God to heal me if it was His will. Somehow, I knew it *was* His will to heal. I just didn't know how to get from that knowledge to the manifestation of my healing.

The thing that changed was that hope came alive in me. I prayed, worshiped God, and threw my heart wide open to His deep desire to help me.

We knew that it was a blood disease that originated in the Middle East. What we didn't know was what to do about it. They determined after bone marrow was taken from my chest that it was terminal and I had five to seven years to live. My spleen had doubled in size because of the disease. To keep me alive, I was admitted to the hospital for a splenectomy.

The surgery had already been scheduled. As I waited in my hospital room, someone tapped on my door and a young woman tiptoed inside. She was a fan of my musical television show. She held a book in her hand. "I hope this book will help you," she said. "I'm praying for you." I thanked her, and she slipped out of the room.

I looked at the book, *I Believe in Miracles* by Kathryn Kuhlman. The book told about miracles of healing in the here and now. I was amazed, and hope began to rise in me. My eyes opened for the first time to the world of miracles.

My surgeon had a conflict in his schedule so my surgery was postponed for a couple of days. I was discharged and sent home to wait. Back at home, I read more stories about Jesus' healing power in the Gospels. I still remember the scriptural sequence. I first read about the woman with the issue of blood (Mark 5:25-34).

All the woman had done was *say* that if she could only touch the hem of Jesus' garment she would be healed. It happened just the way she said it would. My faith took another leap forward.

Jesus the Same Today

The next scripture I read was the story of the lame beggar at the Gate Beautiful located in Acts 3:1-11. What a dramatic scene as Peter and John imparted a miracle to him. I soaked it in, my whole body experiencing power that I'd never experienced before. I said in my heart, *This is so awesome. I only wish it could be for today.*

Then I read Hebrews 13:8, "Jesus Christ the same yesterday, today, and forever." Two words lit up like a neon sign: *same today, same today, same today.* Over and over, I repeated those words like a chant. "Same today! Same today! Same today!"

That was it. I jumped up and danced around the room, crying and praising God. It *is* God's will for me *today. Right now. It's already done!*

That revelation hit me so hard that it knocked me to the floor.

I couldn't move a muscle. I felt like both boiling water and cold water were circulating through my body, particularly through my blood vessels. After about 30 minutes, I stopped vibrating and stood up. I was completely whole.

I knew I'd been healed.

I called my doctor and told him what had happened. I was told to come to his office for an evaluation. When I arrived, he had me lie on my back on the exam table as he palpated my spleen. The doctor pushed harder and harder, and then stopped.

"Your spleen is completely normal!" The expression on his face was a mixture of shock and joy. They took a blood sample and sent me home.

"I'll call you as soon as we figure this out," he said as I left.

Three days later, at about midnight, I'd just drifted off to sleep when the phone rang.

It was my personal physician. "We've done every test we know how to do, and we can't find any trace of the disease. We don't read about these things in our medical books."

"Doctor," I answered, "there's a book where you can read about these things on every page. It's the Bible, the Word of God."

I was so grateful for Kathryn Kuhlman's book that I wrote a personal letter to her at her Pittsburgh ministry office. I told her my story and thanked her for her book. Within a week, we received a phone call from Maggie, her assistant. She invited Cathy and me to spend a whole day with Miss Kuhlman. We set up a time and made that divine appointment.

A few days later, Maggie called again. She asked if I would share my testimony and sing on Miss Kuhlman's television program, "I Believe in Miracles." She also asked if I would join her for several of her large meetings across the United States.

I was scheduled to appear on her television program and had booked my ticket. When it came time to leave, I had the flu, with all its symptoms. I boarded the plane and used the air sickness bag on the trip to Los Angeles. I made it to my hotel and fell into bed, still nauseated and weak. I was so embarrassed to be sick as I arrived in California to give my healing testimony!

At six o'clock the next morning, the phone in my hotel room rang. I answered it in a fog. It was Miss Kuhlman. I recognized her voice as she said in her very musical way, "Good morning, Len."

The power of God through those three words came through the telephone and knocked me across the room and onto the floor. When I stood up, I was totally healed. That's the kind of power that she carried.

As you read this book you will discover that I spend quite a bit of time on the floor! But each time I fall I get up healed, renewed, stronger, and with clear direction.

A while later, I was driven to CBS Studios where she recorded her show. It was the same studio where Carol Burnett and other people recorded their programs. I rehearsed with Dino Kartsonakis, went to make-up, and then waited for her to arrive.

The Wind of God

Without warning, the heavy background curtain in the studio flew up as though a burst of wind had hit it. One of the cameramen turned to me, "She just entered the building."

"How do you know?" I asked.

"That curtain moves like that every time she enters the building."

Of course, no direct air flow is allowed in a sound stage, in order to avoid wind noise or curtain movement. In a minute or less, Miss Kuhlman burst through the door. She greeted everyone, and we recorded the show.

I left the building wondering what kind of power she carried that could cause a curtain to move on another floor. It was supernatural; there was no natural explanation.

Over the following months, I joined her in several of her meetings and watched God do miraculous and inexplicable things too numerous to mention. Once her meetings started, she never left the stage. My greatest challenge in working with her was staying on my feet.

She moved in almost ballet-style worship movements, circling me as she praised Jesus. As I sang, my knees buckled under the weight of the glory of God. His presence was powerful, and I witnessed things difficult to comprehend with the natural mind.

There are dozens of stories and experiences I could share. Suffice it to say, that Kathryn Kuhlman was a very unusual person, who refused to put God in a box. I'd experienced my own healing miracle, confirmed by physicians.

In her meetings, I witnessed hundreds of dramatic healings. I watched as thousands gave their lives to Christ.

The thing that set her apart was not only her faith in God, but her deep worship. She worshiped so much and kept such an intimate relationship with the Holy Spirit that she almost wore His presence like a garment. That's what blew the curtains up when she entered the building.

Her goal in ministry was to win souls. Kathryn Kuhlman never longed for a healing ministry. She became such a conduit for the presence of God that people were healed just from being near her.

The Glory of His Presence

Why am I telling you this? Because there is nothing more wonderful than a lifestyle of praise and worship. That's why so many people sat in Kathryn Kuhlman's meetings and received healing without prayer. Amazing things happen when you live a life of intimacy with the Holy Spirit.

When I ministered with Miss Kuhlman in those early days, I hadn't had the revelation of the crossfire. I didn't know how the angels circled the throne of God and shouted, "Holy! Holy! Holy!" Now, looking back on those times with her, I understand why I had a hard time standing. I understand why miracles happened with no one asking. Her worship created the atmosphere that drew God's presence and attracted miracles.

Living a life of praise and worship will generate miracles to you and through you.

The benefits of developing a life of intimacy with God are accessible to everyone, regardless of age, gender, background, ethnicity, education, or position in life.

Worship transcends circumstances. It builds character and moral fortitude. It fosters better decisions in every area of life. It strengthens your connections with God, severing toxic patterns. It elevates your emotions and strengthens you spiritually, physically, mentally, and emotionally.

Worship promotes unity on every level of marriage. It promotes peace and a sense of well-being. It instills in us a sense of destiny. It attracts favor with both God and man.

Worship gives parents a strong sense of divine order, not only to help children create healthy self-esteem, but to clarify the connection between actions and consequences.

Worship improves confidence, peace, and a sense of purpose. It frees you from condemnation.

Worship possesses frequencies that bypass your minds to express the Holy Spirit.

Praise and worship help overthrow addictions.

Praise and worship awaken your heart to God's voice.

Praise and worship contribute to long life and build physical and emotional strength.

Aggressive, focused praise is a strong weapon of warfare. It causes Satan a lot of pain because he isn't receiving the adoration that he craves. It flushes out negative, toxic thinking. It keeps your focus on God's grace, love and promises.

Praise and worship open the windows of heaven over you.

Praise and worship enthrone God and dethrone self.

In praise and worship you discover that divine frequencies embedded in music can change anything. They can overcome adverse circumstances and hardships.

Praise and worship help to develop a lifestyle of gratitude.

So, how do you get started on this amazing journey with God?

Here's an idea. Go outside. Look up at the night sky. Throw your heart wide open, and join the cosmic chorus of praise!

LEN MINK

Len Mink has been an acclaimed vocalist since his teenage years. He was invited to be the guest artist by the Cincinnati Symphony Orchestra for over thirty-two Pop Concerts. Len had his own syndicated CBS television show and made guest appearances on NBC's Tonight Show and many others. Through his intensive study of sound and the power of musical frequencies, he turned his attention to the Creator and has become a beloved worship leader around the world.

Let it Rain

A deeply stirring worship experience designed to carry you into an intimate encounter with God. Step into His presence with Len Mink at his very best!

Redemption

Let your spirit soar with the rich sounds of a full symphony orchestra and choir plus the heavenly tones of Stradivarius violins. Featuring beautiful hymns as well as newer selections, the orchestration and arrangements are overwhelming as God's Spirit flows through Len's beautiful voice, bringing glory to our God. A must for your sacred music library.

www.lenandcathymink.com
1-800-426-5766

Let The Praise Begin

Smooth songs of worship in a variety of styles and tempos bring victory to hearts every day. The song duo "Faith/I Win," will have you shouting, "I'm not quitting, I'm a winner!" And the beautiful "Agnus Dei" takes you to the throne worshipping the King of Kings and Lord of Lords.

Under The Shadow

The smooth tones of Len's voice put this CD at the top of the chart in popularity! The lead song, "Under The Shadow," beautifully declares the divine protection of the 91st Psalm. Worshipful and comforting, it also features the all time favorites, "Shout To The Lord" and "Welcome Holy Spirit." Reports of healings while listening to this project are numerous.

www.lenandcathymink.com
1-800-426-5766

NOTES

1. "Double slit experiment in a hall of mirrors: A purely quantum physical variation of the classic experiment with two atoms reveals surprising interference phenomena," MAX-PLANCKGESELLSCHAFT, https://www.mpg.de/10380030/double-slit-experiment-atoms, (March 21, 2016)

2. Capps, Annette. *Quantum Faith.* Capps Publishing. England, Ark. 2006.

3. Ibid. p.15-18.

4. Quotes, Quotable Quotes, Goodreads, https://www.goodreads.com/quotes/95683-whathttps://www.goodreads.com/quotes/95683-what-people-have-the-capacity-to-choose-they-have-thepeople-have-the-capacity-to-choose-they-have-the accessed April 30, 2019

5. Letters of Note, "Helen Keller's Letter to the New York Symphony Orchestra," http://www.lettersofnote.com/2014/03/my-heart-almost-stood-still.html (March 27, 2014).

6. Stephen Hawking, *The Illustrated A Brief History of Time* (New York; Bantam, 1006) 156.

7. Peplow, Mark. "Hawking changes his mind about black holes." July 15, 2004. https://www.nature.com/news/2004/040712/full/040712-12.html

8. George Sylvester Viereck, "What Life Means to Einstein," *Saturday Evening Post,* October 26, 1929.

9. Bill McQuay and Christopher Joyce, "How Sound Shaped the Evolution of Your Brain," *National Public Radio,* September

10, 2015 https://www.npr.org/sections/healthhttps://www.npr.
org/sections/health-shots/2015/09/10/436342537/how-sound-
shaped-the-evolution-of-your-brainshots/2015/09/10/436342537/
how-sound-shaped-the-evolution-of-your-brain

10. "Close Listening: Decoding Nature Through Sound," *Morning Edition's
Summer Series*. Sounds of the Bayaka https://www.npr.org/sections/
health-shots/2015/09/10/436342537/how-soundhttps://www.npr.org/
sections/healthshots/2015/09/10/436342537/how-sound-shaped-the-evo-
lution-of-your-brainshaped-the-evolution-of-your-brain

11. "Close Listening: Decoding Nature Through Sound," *Morning
Edition's Summer Series*. The Sound Everyone Hates. https://
www.npr.org/sections/health-shots/2015/09/10/436342537/
how-sound-shaped-the-evolution-of-your-brain

12. "Close Listening: Decoding Nature Through Sound," *Morning Edition's
Summer Series*. Sound of a Frog's Brain. https://www.npr.org/sections/
health-shots/2015/09/10/436342537/howhttps://www.npr.org/sections/
health-shots/2015/09/10/436342537/how-sound-shaped-the-evolution-
of-your-brainsound-shaped-the-evolution-of-your-brain

13. Phonation Physiology, *Quizlet* https://quizlet.com/126696354/
phonation-physiology-flashhttps://quizlet.com/126696354/
phonation-physiology-flash-cards/cards/

14. Meghan Holohan, "Unborn babies are hearing you,
loud and clear" *Today*. https://www.today.com/parents/
unborn-babies-are-hearing-you-loud-clear-8C11005474

15. Jacques Mehler, Josiane Bertoncini, Michele Barriere, "Infant
Recognition of Mother's Voice" *Perception*. 1978. volume 7. P. 491-497

16. Anton St. Maarten, Quotes, Goodreads. https://www.goodreads.com/quotes/8632178-selfhttps://www.goodreads.com/quotes/8632178-self-pity-is-spiritual-suicide-it-is-an-indefensible-self-mutilation-ofpity-is-spiritual-suicide-it-is-an-indefensible-self-mutilation-of

17. Rick Renner, "Why Do People Sometimes Collapse in the Presence of God?" August 22, 2019 https://renner.org/devotionals/why-do-people-sometimes-collapse-in-the-presence-of-god/

18. Picture Quotes, A. W. Tozer, "True and absolute freedom is only found in the presence of God" IdleHearts, https://www.idlehearts.com/982806/true-and-absolute-freedom-is-onlyhttps://www.idlehearts.com/982806/true-and-absolute-freedom-is-only-found-in-the-presence-of-godfound-in-the-presence-of-god

19. Faucett's Bible Dictionary, Definition of Seraphim. 1878. https://www.biblehttps://www.bible-history.com/faussets/history.com/faussets/

20. The Supernova Cosmology Project, High-Z Supernova Search Team. https://www.cfa.harvard.edu/supernova/HighZ.html

21. "'Every Praise': Kidnapper Releases 10-Year-Old Who Won't Stop Singing Gospel Song," Fox Insider, August 22, 2014 https://insider.foxnews.com/2014/04/22/%E2%80%98everyhttps://insider.foxnews.com/2014/04/22/%E2%80%98every-praise%E2%80%99-kidnapper-releases-10-year-old-who-won%E2%80%99t-stop-singing-gospel-songpraise%E2%80%99-kidnapper-releases-10-year-old-who-won%E2%80%99t-stop-singing-gospelhttps://insider.foxnews.com/2014/04/22/%E2%80%98every-praise%E2%80%99-kidnapper-releases-10-year-old-who-won%E2%80%99t-stop-singing-gospel-song-song

22. Bryant Wood. "The Walls of Jericho: Archeology Confirms: They Really Did Come A-tumblin' Down" *Answers in Genesis.* March 1, 1999. https://answersingenesis.org/archaeology/thehttps://answersingenesis.org/archaeology/the-walls-of-jericho/walls-of-jericho/

23. Reynald Francisco, "The Fall of Jericho: From an Engineer's Perspective," *My Own Daily Bread,* August 20,2009, http://myown-dailybread.blogspot.com/2009/08/fall-of-jericho-fromhttp://myown-dailybread.blogspot.com/2009/08/fall-of-jericho-from-engineers.htmlengineers.html

24. Vaushnavi Patil, "Can a Contingent Of Marching Soldiers Collapse A Bridge?" *ScienceABC,* https://www.scienceabc.com/humans/can-a-contingent-of-marching-soldiers-collapse-ahttps://www.scienceabc.com/humans/can-a-contingent-of-marching-soldiers-collapse-a-bridge.htmlbridge.html

25. Ellicott's Commentary for English Readers. Epist.X.96 AdMart.C2.

26. Fackler, Guido: Music in Concentration Camps 1933-1945. In: *Music and Politics.* Online: https://quod.lib.umich.edu/m/mp/9460447.0001.102/--music-in-concentrationcamps1933https://quod.lib.umich.edu/m/mp/9460447.0001.102/musicinconcentra-tioncamps19331945?rgn=main;view=fulltext1945?rgn=main;view=fulltext

27. Ibid.

28. Ibid.

29. Ibid.

30. Ibid.

31. Kalisch, Shoshana. *Yes, We Sang!: Songs of the Ghettos and Concentration Camps*. New York: Harper & Row, c1985

32. CBS SUNDAY. *Special Report*. February 2007

33. Christ, Scott. "20 Surprising Science-backed Health Benefits of Music." *Greatest*. Dec. 12, 2013 https://greatist.com/happiness/unexpected-health-benefits-music

34. Karanam, Ketki. "Can Background Music Boost Cognition?" *Synch Project*. July 20,2016. http://syncproject.co/blog/2016/7/19/can-background-music-boost-cognition

35. Gill, Victoria. "Singing, 'rewires' damaged brain," *BBC News*. Feb. 21, 2010. http://news.bbc.co.uk/2/hi/science/nature/8526699.stm

36. Abrahms, Sally. "Tune In To Music Therapy's Healing Powers." *AARP Bulletin*. March 2013.Vol 54. No.2. https://www.sallyabrahms.com/articles/sally-abrahms-how-music-therapyhttps://www.sallyabrahms.com/articles/sally-abrahms-how-music-therapy-helps-people-heal/helps-people-heal/

37. Larson, Zeb. *Origins: Current Events in Historical Perspective*. April 2018 Vol. 11 Issue 7. https://origins.osu.edu/article/americas-long-suffering-mental-health-system